THE CASE FOR JESUS THE MESSIAH

☆ ☆ ☆ ☆

INCREDIBLE PROPHECIES THAT PROVE GOD EXISTS

John Ankerberg
Dr. John Weldon
Dr. Walter C. Kaiser, Jr.

HARVEST HOUSE PUBLISHERS, INC.
Eugene, Oregon 97402

THE CASE FOR JESUS THE MESSIAH

ACKNOWLEDGEMENT

The authors would especially like to acknowledge and thank the gracious assistance of Mrs. Louise Ebner, M.A., who has diligently sat with us through the evolution of each of our books. She faithfully assists us, page by page, in refining and correcting our manuscripts, including this one. Her spirit and good cheer are a source of constant blessing.

Finally, we would be amiss not to thank two excellent and patient typists, Lynda Lane and Rhonda Spence. These dear ladies are a special blessing from the Lord and a debt of gratitude is owed to them.

CONTENTS

PREFACE

In an interview with famous scientist Albert Einstein in the *Saturday Evening Post*, October 26, 1929, we find the following dialogue:

"To what extent are you influenced by Christianity?"

"As a child I received instruction both in the Bible and in the Talmud. I am a Jew, but I am enthralled by the luminous figure of the Nazarene."

"Have you read Emil Ludwig's book on Jesus?"

"Emil Ludwig's Jesus is shallow. Jesus is too colossal for the pen of phrasemongers, however artful. No man can dispose of Christianity with a *bon mot* [a witty remark]."

"You accept the historical existence of Jesus?"

"Unquestionably! No one can read the Gospels without feeling the actual presence of Jesus. His personality pulsates in every word. No myth is filled with such life."(5:40) *

After the Holocaust Einstein wrote a letter to the Episcopal Bishop Edward R. Wells (reported in the Baltimore Evening Sun, April 13, 1979) in 1945 concerning the behavior of the Church during this time. He stated:

> "Being a lover of freedom...I looked to the universities to defend it, knowing that they had always boasted of their devotion to the cause of truth; but, no, the universities immediately were silenced. Then I looked to the great editors of the newspapers whose flaming editorials in days gone by had proclaimed their love of freedom; but they, like the universities, were silenced in a few short weeks. Only the church stood squarely across the path of Hitler's campaign for suppressing the truth. I never had any special interest in the church before, but now I feel a great affection and admiration because the church alone has had the courage and persistence to stand for intellectual truth and

---

*Throughout this book the numbers in parentheses refer to footnotes and mean the following: the first number always refers to the book in the bibliography with that number. The numbers after the colon refer to the page numbers in the book cited. Where a book has two volumes, we have identified the volume with Roman numeral I or II.

moral freedom. I am forced to confess that what I once despised I now praise unreservedly.''(5:40-41)

Jesus of Nazareth. He shattered the world. Never has there been a man like Him, and never will there be again. He is the subject of more books, more plays, more poetry, more films, and more worship than any man in human history.

Whatever good Christianity has done for the world has come only because of Jesus of Nazareth. But who was this man? The purpose of this book is to show how the Hebrew Scriptures predicted centuries in advance the coming of a divine Messiah for all mankind.

Some have claimed that these statements were made after Jesus lived, not before. Some claim the books of the Hebrew Scriptures were written close to the time of Christ and the Messianic prophecies were merely Christian inventions. But to make such a claim is impossible. The entire Hebrew Scriptures were completed by 400 B.C. and no matter what your view of the Hebrew Scriptures, one fact is unassailable. The Septuagint, the Greek translation of the entire Hebrew Scriptures, was completed by 247 B.C.

Therefore, even critics must acknowledge that every prophecy we will discuss in this book, and many more, were in existence well in advance of the time Jesus lived — in fact, at least some 250 years before He was even born.

We will also show that the Messiah is spoken of in such specific detail in the Hebrew Scriptures that it is literally impossible to account for such predictions apart from the Bible being a divine revelation of God to man.

There are those today who reject this conclusion, but they refuse to consider the prophecies fairly and on their own merit. Often, they mistakenly dismiss them out of hand. But only a preexisting bias against supernatural prophecy itself (such as those holding a *rationalistic* world view) or a bias against these prophecies referring to the Person of Jesus can deter someone from accepting the Scriptures as Messianic prophecy.

We have written this book to set forth a small portion of the evidence found in the Hebrew Scriptures that predicted the coming of the Messiah. We believe God gave this evidence so that those who are willing to allow the facts to speak for themselves will be able to discover the truth.

INTRODUCTION

What We Have Included in This Book

Is there evidence in history that God gave specific information hundreds of years in advance about a person He knew would live? What specific accounts are given and where can they be found? Did the people to whom the information came recognize that they had been given special information? Do these prophecies constitute solid evidence for us today? Is it possible for us to account for this information apart from the fact it must have come from God? Did the Jewish community before and after Christ believe these same Hebrew Scriptures pointed to a coming Messiah?

These prophecies are like clues in a mystery story. In this book we will try to gather enough clues to identify the special person who is talked about in the Hebrew Scriptures. As we shall see, the clues will lead us to ask:

- Who is the seed (offspring) of the woman who crushes the head of Satan?

- Who is the seed of Abraham, Isaac and Jacob that will eventually bless all the nations?

- Who is the "prophet like Moses" of whom God says, "You must listen to him"?

- Who is the One crucified?

- Who is David's "Lord"?

- Who is the child that is God and will have an everlasting kingdom?

- Who was crushed and pierced for our transgressions? Upon whom did the Lord lay the iniquity of all mankind?

- Who is the righteous Branch, the wise King, who will be called "the Lord our righteousness"?

- Who is the "Anointed One" to be "cut off" after 483 years?

- Who is the One who is eternal, who will be the ruler over Israel, who is born in Bethlehem Ephrathah?

- Who is the King of Jerusalem, "righteous and having salvation" who comes "gentle and riding on a donkey"?

- Who is Jehovah, "the One they have pierced" for whom Jerusalem and all the nation of Israel will weep and mourn?

- When did God suddenly come to His temple? Who was the messenger He sent before Him to prepare the way?

The Bible claims to be the unique revelation of God. *"All Scripture is given by inspiration of God, and is profitable for doctrine, for reproof, for correction, for instruction in righteousness; that the man of God may be perfect, thoroughly furnished unto all good works"* (2 Tim. 3:16, 17). If you do not agree, the material discussed in this book should be of interest to you. The Bible's claim to uniqueness and the prophecies of a future Messiah go together. If the prophecies are truly fulfilled, then the Bible has given information about the future that could only have come from God. Our goal will be to examine a handful of the many prophetic statements and explain why anyone who looks at the clear meaning of the words will realize these verses all point to a future Person.

We will also explain the text and the context. After that, we will see if there is evidence that a number of Jewish rabbis accepted these passages as Messianic.

Finally, we will ask if this specific information finds fulfillment in any other person but Jesus Christ.

When examining this evidence we are aware that some people have applied different interpretations to these verses. We are aware of the disagreements but are convinced they are the result of misinterpretation or biased assumptions that will not allow the evidence to speak for itself (e.g., 10/24/54). In the last chapters of this book we will answer some of the frequent objections that have been made by scholars.

We have also included important appendices on the historical fact of the resurrection and the virgin birth of Christ. The last appendix was written by Dr. Walter Kaiser, Professor of Semitic Languages and Old Testament and Dean of Trinity Evangelical Divinity School in Deerfield, Illinois.

But before we examine the specific prophecies and answer the critics, we want to document the amazing fact that in the Bible God did promise to give information through His prophets concerning the future.

Jesus said, "How foolish are you, and how slow of heart to believe all that *the prophets* have spoken! Did not *the Christ [Messiah] have to suffer these things* and *then enter His glory?* And beginning with *Moses* and *all the Prophets,* He explained to them what was said in *all the Scriptures* concerning *Himself*" (Lk. 24:25-57).

The Apostle Peter wrote, "The things which *God announced* beforehand by the mouth of *all the prophets,* that His *Christ* [Messiah] should *suffer,* He has thus fulfilled" (Acts 3:18).

"[If we examine] those passages in the Old Testament to which the ancient synagogue referred as Messianic . . . [we find] upwards of 456...and their Messianic application is supported by more than 558 references to the most ancient rabbinic writings . . . A careful perusal of their Scripture quotations show, that *the main postulates of the New Testament concerning the Messiah are fully supported by rabbinic statements.*" — Alfred Edersheim, a teacher of languages and Warbutonian Lecturer at Lincoln's Inn (Oxford); Grinfield Lecturer on the Septuagint. (47:I,163-164, emphasis added)

1. Did God Promise to Speak Through His Prophets Things Concerning the Future?

The Biblical Text

*"Who then is like me? Let him proclaim it. Let him declare and lay out before me what has happened . . . and what is yet to come – yes, let him foretell what will come . . . **Did I not proclaim this and foretell it long ago?"** (Isa. 44:7, 8, emphasis added)*

God promised to speak through His prophets and said this would be proof that He was God; indeed the true God for all the earth. He even challenged one and all to make statements about the future that would be as accurate as His statements about the future.

It is significant that in the most Messianic of all the Hebrew Scriptures, Isaiah, God speaks most frequently of His ability to predict the future. He challenges the false gods (idols) and their prophets to prove their case.

For example:

*"Declare to us **the things to come**, tell us what the future holds, so that we may know that you are gods." (Isa. 41:23)*

*"Who **foretold this long ago**, who declared it from the distant past? Was it not I, the Lord?" (Isa. 45:21)*

*"**I foretold** the former things long ago, my mouth announced them and I made them known; then suddenly I acted, and they came to pass . . . . Therefore I told you these things long ago; **before they happened** I announced them to you so that you could not say, 'My idols did them.'" (Isa. 48:3,5)*

"Above all, you must understand that no prophecy of Scripture came about by the prophet's own interpretation. For prophecy never had its origin

*in the will of man, **but men spoke from God** as they were carried along by His Holy Spirit."* (1 Pet. 1:20-22)

*"**All the prophets testify about Him** that everyone who believes in Him receives forgiveness of sins through His name."* (Acts 10:43)

*". . . So I stand here and testify to small and great alike. I am saying nothing beyond what **the prophets and Moses said** would happen – that the Christ [Messiah] would suffer and, as the first to rise from the dead, would proclaim light to His own people and to the Gentiles."* (Acts 26:22,23; emphasis added in the above verses)

Concerning this last statement that the prophets and Moses spoke about the Messiah, in the next chapter we will learn what people usually meant when they used the word and spoke about the "Messiah."

2. Definition of the Word "Messiah"

The term "Messiah" is taken from Psalm 2:2 and Daniel 9:25,26 where *Mashiach* (Heb.); *Messias* (Gk.) means "Anointed One." The term took its meaning from the Jewish practice of "anointing" prophets, priests and kings to their respective offices. As a generic term it could be applied to an earthly king such as David (2 Sam. 19:21) who was "anointed" to fulfill the divine purpose of his office.

However, there was one unique individual to whom the term "Messiah" applied in a special sense. God spoke about a future Ruler of Israel who would sit on the throne of David and usher in an age of righteousness and peace. He would simultaneously hold all three offices of prophet (authoritative proclamation), priest (spiritual duties) and king (political ruler). He would be the reality and ultimate fulfillment to which all other usages of the term "Messiah" would be but shadowy pre-figures. (52:II, 50-53)

He would be the One to come whom God would uniquely identify beforehand. As the Apostle Peter said, *"But this is how God fulfilled **what He had foretold** through all the prophets, saying that His Christ [Messiah] would suffer"* (Acts 3:18, emphasis added).

Before we examine in detail the prophecies the Bible claims God made through the prophets identifying the Messiah, we want to ask – "What would it prove if such statements about a future Messiah were given and actually fulfilled many years later in one person?"

3. If Specific Prophecies Were Fulfilled by the Messiah, Does the Science of Probability Consider This Proof There Is a God?

Anyone can *make* predictions – that is easy. Having them fulfilled is another story entirely. The more statements you make about the future and the greater the detail, the better the chances are that you will be proven wrong.

For example, think how difficult it would be for someone to predict the exact city in which the birth of a future U.S. President would take place in the year 2689 A.D. But that's what the prophet Micah did 700 years before the Messiah.

How difficult do you think it would be to indicate the precise kind of death that a new, unknown religious leader would experience a thousand years from today? Could you invent and predict now a new method of execution not currently known – one that won't even be invented for hundreds of years? That's what David did in 1000 B.C. when he wrote Psalm 22.

Or, how difficult would it be to predict the specific date of the appearance of some great future leader hundreds of years in advance? But that's what the prophet Daniel did 530 years before Christ.

On the other hand, if you did think up 50 specific prophecies about some man in the future you will never meet, how difficult do you think it would be for that man to fulfill all 50 of your predictions? How hard would it be for him if 25 of your predictions were about what other people would do to him and were completely beyond his control?

For example*, how could someone "arrange" to be born in a specific family? How does someone "arrange" in advance to have his parents give birth to him in a specified city, not their own? How does one "arrange" to be virgin born? How does one "arrange" to

*In the prophecies below we have given references when they are not discussed in the body of the text.

16

be considered a prophet "like Moses"? How does someone "arrange" (a) his own death, including being put to death by the strange method of crucifixion, (b) being put to death, not alone, but with company, specifically two criminals and (c) then "arrange" to have his executioners gamble for his clothes during the execution?

And how does one "arrange" to have God inform and send the proper "messenger" to go before one? How does one "arrange" to be betrayed for a specific amount of money (30 pieces of silver) How does one "arrange" in advance that his executioners will carry out their regular practice of breaking the legs of the two victims on either side of him, but not his? Finally, how does a pretender to being the Messiah "arrange" to be God? How does he escape from a grave and appear to people after he has been killed?

It might be possible to fake one or two of these, but it would be impossible for any man to arrange and fulfill all these predictions in advance. If it can be proved that such statements (prophecies) were predicted of the Messiah hundreds of years in advance, and one man fulfilled *all* of them, then that man would logically have to be the Messiah.

God gave a great number of prophecies about the Messiah for at least two reasons. First, it would make identifying the Messiah obvious. And second, it would make an imposter's task impossible.

To illustrate, the following account is a true story of how governments use prearranged identification signs to identify correct agents. It's taken from the *New Leader* of April 2, 1951.

David Greenglass was a World War II traitor. He gave atomic secrets to the Russians and then fled to Mexico after the war. His conspirators arranged to help him by planning a meeting with the secretary of the Russian ambassador in Mexico City. Proper identification for both parties became vital.

Greenglass was to identify himself with six prearranged signs. These instructions had been given to both the secretary and

Greenglass so there would be no possibility of making a mistake. They were: (1) once in Mexico City Greenglass was to write a note to the secretary, signing his name as "I. Jackson"; (2) after three days he was to go to the Plaza de Colon in Mexico City and (3) stand before the statue of Columbus, (4) with his middle finger placed in a guide book. In addition, (5) when he was approached, he was to say it was a magnificent statue and that he was from Oklahoma. (6) The secretary was to then give him a passport.

The six prearranged signs worked. Why? With six identifying characteristics it was impossible for the secretary not to identify Greenglass as the proper contact. (16:43)

If that is true, think how impossible it would be not to identify the Messiah if he had been given 456 identifying characteristics. (47:163, 164; 710-741)

One final thing must be said. If we assume 456 prophecies are fulfilled in one person, what does the science of probability say about this? In brief, it says, if accurate predictions were made about a future Messiah and fulfilled years later by one person, this is proof that there is a God.

Here is why. The science of probability attempts to determine the chance that a given event will occur. The value and accuracy of the science of probability has been established beyond doubt. For example, probability statistics are the foundation on which all kinds of insurance rates are fixed.

Professor Emeritus of Science at Westmont College, Peter Stoner, has calculated the probability of one man fulfilling the major prophecies made concerning the Messiah. The estimates were worked out by twelve different classes of 600 college students.

The students carefully weighed all the factors, discussed each prophecy at length, and examined the various circumstances which might indicate that men had conspired together to fulfill a particular prophecy. They made their estimates conservative enough so that there was finally unanimous agreement even among the most skeptical students.

But then Professor Stoner took their estimates and made them even more conservative. He also encouraged other skeptics or scientists to make their own estimates to see if his conclusions were more than fair. Finally, he submitted his figures for review to a Committee of the American Scientific Affiliation. Upon examination, they verified that his calculations were dependable and accurate in regard to the scientific material presented. (19:4)

For example, concerning Micah 5:2, where it states the Messiah would be born in Bethlehem Ephrathah, Stoner and his students determined the *average* population of Bethlehem from the time of Micah to the present; then they divided it by the *average* population of the earth during the same period. They concluded that the chance of one man being born in Bethlehem was one in 2.8×10^5 – or rounded, one in 300,000.

After examining eight different prophecies, they conservatively estimated that the chance of one man fulfilling all eight prophecies was one in 10^{17}.

To illustrate how large the number 10^{17} is (a figure with 17 zeros), Stoner gave this illustration. Imagine covering the entire state of Texas with silver dollars to a level of two feet deep. The total number of silver dollars needed to cover the whole state would be 10^{17}. Now, choose just one of those silver dollars, mark it and drop it from an airplane. Then thoroughly stir all the silver dollars all over the state.

When that has been done, blindfold one man, tell him he can travel wherever he wishes in the state of Texas. But sometime he must stop, reach down into the two feet of silver dollars and try to pull up that one specific silver dollar that has been marked.

Now, the chance of his finding that one silver dollar in the state of Texas would be the chance the prophets had for eight of their prophecies coming true in any one man in the future.

In financial terms, is there anyone who would not invest in a financial venture if the chance of failure were only one in 10^{17}? This is the kind of sure investment we are offered by God for belief in His Messiah.

19

Professor Stoner concluded: "The fulfillment of these eight prophecies alone proves that God inspired the writing of those prophecies to a definiteness which lacks only one chance in 10^{17} of being absolute." (19:107)

Another way of saying this is that any person who minimizes or ignores the significance of the biblical identifying signs concerning the Messiah would be foolish.

But, of course, there are many more than eight prophecies. In another calculation Stoner used 48 prophecies (even though he could have used 456) and arrived at the extremely conservative estimate that the probability of 48 prophecies being fulfilled in one person is 10^{157} (19:109).

How large is the number one in 10^{157}? 10^{157} contains 157 zeros! Let us try to illustrate this number using electrons.

Electrons are very small objects. They are smaller than atoms. It would take 2.5 times 10^{15} of them, laid side by side, to make one inch. Even if we counted four electrons every second and counted day and night, it would still take us 19 million years just to count a line of electrons one-inch long.

But how many electrons would it take if we were dealing with 10^{157} electrons? Imagine building a solid ball of electrons that would extend in all directions from the earth a length of 6 billion light years. The distance in miles of just *one* light year is 6.4 trillion miles. That would be a big ball! But not big enough to measure 10^{157} electrons.

In order to do that, you must take that big ball of electrons reaching the length of 6 billion light years long in all directions and multiply it by 6×10^{28}! How big is that? It's the length of the space required to store trillions and trillions and trillions of the same gigantic balls and more. In fact, the space required to store all of these balls combined together would just start to "scratch the surface" of the number of electrons we would need to really accurately speak about 10^{157}.

But assuming you have some idea of the number of electrons we are talking about, now imagine marking just one of those electrons in that huge number. Stir them all up. Then appoint one person to travel in a rocket for as long as he wants, anywhere he wants to go. Tell him to stop and segment a part of space, then take a high-powered microscope and find that one marked electron in that segment. What do you think his chances of being successful would be? It would be one in 10^{157}.

Remember, this number represents the chance of only 48 prophecies coming true in one person. It illustrates why it is absolutely impossible for anyone to have fulfilled all the Messianic prophecies by chance. In fact, a leading authority on probability theory, Emile Borel, states in his book *Probabilities and Life*, that once we go past one chance in 10^{50}, the probabilities are so small it's impossible to think they will ever occur. (34)

Here is one last illustration of the immensity of the number 10^{157} and why the science of probability shows we are dealing with the miraculous. Imagine one ant traveling at the speed of only *one inch* every 15 billion years. If he could only carry one atom at a time, how many atoms could he move in 10^{157} years? He could, even at that incredibly slow speed, be able to move all the atoms in 600,000 trillion, trillion, trillion, trillion universes the size of our universe, a distance of 30 billion light years! (50:120)

Again, all of this means it is impossible for 48 prophecies to be fulfilled by chance. It is proof that there must be a God who supernaturally gave this information. The question is, can it be shown that such prophecies do exist?

We will now examine 13 prophetic passages that give us specific statements about the Messiah. As you read through them, ask yourself the following questions. Is this truly a prophecy about a future person? Does Jesus Christ fulfill it? How was it possible for each of these prophecies to find fulfillment in one man hundreds of years in the future? If each prophecy is admitted to be about the Messiah and Jesus Christ fulfills one prophecy after another, isn't this proof that Jesus is the Messiah?

For the sake of clarity, we have translated some passages from the Hebrew; for others we have cited the NIV or the NAS.

21

4. Genesis 3:15 – Who Is the Seed (Offspring) of the Woman Who Crushes the Head of Satan?

The Biblical Text

"So the Lord God said to the serpent, 'Because you have done this, . . . I will put enmity between you and the woman, and between your seed and her seed. He will bruise your head, and you will bruise his heel.'" (Gen. 3:14, 15)

The Context of the Passage

The context of this passage is the temptation and Fall of Adam and Eve by the deception of "the serpent." Who is "the serpent"? Revelation 12:9 and 20:2 identifies him as *"the serpent of old, who is the devil or Satan."*

For those who accept only the Hebrew Scriptures as authoritative, the serpent in Genesis 3:14 cannot be just an animal. The *serpent* must be a *person*. The word "enmity" in the Hebrew Scriptures *always* refers to hatred between *persons*. (77:164) It is never used between an animal and a person.

In this passage Satan has already deceived Adam and Eve. All three are now addressed by God. What God says is astonishing!

The Explanation of the Text

Carefully examining this text, we find a number of things:

- God is speaking to the serpent, who is not an animal and is identified in the book of Revelation as "Satan."

- God says He will put enmity (irreconcilable hatred) between the serpent [Satan] and the woman.

22

- God says this enmity will spread to the serpent's seed and the woman's seed. Again, the word "enmity" is a very specialized word. It is never used between an animal and another animal or between an animal and people. It only describes a condition of hatred between persons. (1:39; 76:145)
- But then God suddenly speaks specifically of "one" of Eve's seed, a "he," a male descendant. God announces this One, "He," will someday bruise the head of the serpent (Satan), and Satan will bruise his heel.

The KJV version has made a mistake in translation here. The translators ignored the third person masculine, singular pronoun found in the text and instead of translating the pronoun "he," they mistranslated the pronoun as "it." But the grammar clearly indicates "he." The KJV wrongly says, "*It* shall bruise thy head," the Hebrew says, "*He* will bruise thy head."

So there are five participants spoken of in this verse:

1. Satan

2. the woman

3. Satan's seed

4. the woman's seed

5. finally, from the woman's seed, the "he" who bruises Satan's head but is bruised in the heel by Satan.

Among these five participants, God says there will be, first of all, conflict that takes place and reaches into the future. The conflict will result from enmity (hatred) between Satan and the woman. Second, this hatred will extend to Satan's seed and the woman's seed. Third, someday the woman's seed, One specifically – a "he" – will victoriously defeat Satan by bruising his head; yet Satan will bruise his heel.

What does it mean for the male descendant of the woman to "bruise" Satan's head? Translators have rendered the Hebrew word "bruise" as "crush." (77:166) This is because it more clearly fits

23

both the meaning of the word and the context. The actual Hebrew word means to "break or smite in pieces; greatly to injure or wound." (76:57)

Though the same Hebrew word is used (both the head and heel are "crushed"), we see that one of the wounds is irreversibly fatal, the other is not. Why? The reason is the *location* of the crushing. The crushing of the head is irreparable – it is too vital an organ to survive being crushed. But this is not true for the heel. To crush someone's heel is to inflict a serious but not irreparable wound.

If a man steps on a snake's *head*, it will be irreversibly crushed – thus the imagery points to the serpent's wound as being fatal. On the other hand, a crushed *heel* may be nursed back to health. This is why the great Hebrew scholar Franz Delitzsch has said this verse is teaching "the definite promise of victory over the serpent . . . because it suffers the deadly tread." (52:I,36) In brief, God is saying the male seed of the woman will be victorious over Satan – because he (the serpent) will be mortally wounded.

Does the male descendant here refer to the Messiah? Yes. Many Jewish rabbis have stated so down through the ages. (See the next subheading.) For Adam and Eve it represented a future Person who would conquer the one who had deceived them and led them into sin.

But does Eve's male descendant in this verse refer to the person of Jesus Christ? It is clear that it must refer to some future man and as we will see, God Himself will add other identifying signs to answer this question. Jesus does fit the requirements spoken of here. Jesus Himself said that He had come to destroy the works of the devil (Jn. 12:31; 16:11, cf. Heb. 2:14; 1 Jn. 3:8). Has anyone else in human history ever made such a claim? When Jesus died on the cross, He provided and made available salvation for all mankind (Jn. 3:16). He broke the power Satan had exercised over all humanity, and now provides victory over sin and the devil. Because of Jesus' death on the cross and His resurrection, He inflicted a fatal blow to the devil's domination over man (Acts 10:38; 26:15-18;

Eph. 4:8; Col. 2:15; Js. 4:7). In the future, at Jesus' second coming, He will permanently defeat the devil by removing him from the earth and casting him into hell forever (Rom. 16:20; Rev. 20:10).

The text also talks of the seed (offspring) of the serpent and the seed (offspring) of the woman.

The offspring of Satan would refer to the demons (fallen angels who followed Satan in his rebellion). All through Scripture we are told "Satan's seed" tries to destroy humanity (Jn. 8:44; Rev. 12:9; 16:14). The "seed of the woman" obviously would refer to all her children, to all humanity.*

God describes the scope of the conflict. It will involve all future generations *"between your (Satan's) seed and her (the woman's) seed"* (1 Pet. 5:8; 1 Jn. 5:19).

Satan's success in deceiving Adam and Eve resulted in their spiritual separation from God (Gen. 3:8, 21-24). This verse says Satan will continue to deceive and wreck havoc on the seed of the woman and all humanity (Rev. 12:9; 20:2,3). Yet in the future, God promises a male descendant of the woman will crush and defeat Satan and his seed.

Is not this the Gospel message? Didn't Jesus say He had come to give His life a ransom for many and to destroy the works of Satan (Mt. 20:28; Jn. 12:31; 16:11), to proclaim release to the captives, to set free those who are downtrodden (Lk. 4:18)? In other words, this text is already speaking of Jesus, the Savior, who would come to reverse the destructive works of Satan on all of humanity.

Was Genesis 3:15 Recognized by the Jews as Messianic?

Was this text recognized by the Jews as a Messianic prophecy? The answer is "yes." The words themselves forced Jewish scholars to a Messianic application.

Dr. Charles Feinberg, Professor of Semitics and Old Testament at Talbot Seminary, has documented that, "There has never been a

There is also a reference to the conflict between the human followers of Satan or Christ who have either one or the other as their respective spiritual heads (Mt. 23:33; Jn. 8:44; Gal. 3.26-29, Eph. 4.15, 1 Jn. 3.1,8, 5.19).

time, from ancient days to the present, when the Messianic interpretation of Genesis 3:15 has not had its able advocates." (6:22)

In the Jewish community, the Targum Pseudo-Jonathan on Genesis 3:15 stands as proof that the ancient rabbis (at least at the time of this Targum) believed the words in this verse referred to "the days of the King, Messiah." (71:122)

The same can be said for the Jerusalem Targum. (47:II, 711; 6:22-23) (The *Targumim* (pl.) are ancient Aramaic paraphrases of the Hebrew Bible. The best known are the *Targum Onkelos* [3rd century A.D., on the *Torah*, the first five books of Moses], the *Targum Jonathan* [4th century A.D., on the Prophets], the *Targum Pseudo-Jonathan* [650 A.D., on the *Torah]* and the *Jerusalem Targum* [700 A.D., on the *Torah*].)* And other scholars have "demonstrated beyond a shadow of a doubt, on philological [language] grounds, 'that the Jewish community – at least the one in Alexandria, interpreted this passage as Messianic well before [in 247 B.C.] the birth of Christ.'" (1:42)

In his *Exposition of Genesis*, the renowned Old Testament scholar H. C. Leupold observes that, "The Jewish church, according to the *Targum*, regarded this passage as Messianic from a very early day." (77:170)

Clues to Identify the Messiah

Whoever the Messiah is, He *must* fit the following description:

Clue #1 – He, a male child (the Hebrew text specifically uses a 3rd person, singular, masculine pronoun – "he"), will be born of the seed of the woman.

*Although the Targums are dated A.D., Ellison makes an important observation in his **The Centrality of the Messianic Idea for the Old Testament**: "Early [pre-Christian] rabbinic Messianic interpretation merits re-examination. Very much of their interpretation of Messianic prophecy is, allowing for the difference created by the rejection or acceptance of Jesus as Messiah, the same as that of the New Testament and early Church . . . . Because the influence of Hebrew Christian propaganda, which must have been felt for at least two centuries after the resurrection, has been underestimated by most modern scholars, we have failed to realize how impossible it will have been for the rabbis to adopt Christian interpretations of prophecy, unless indeed they had been there all the time . . . . By the middle of the third century Hebrew Christianity had lost its dynamic power and was rapidly becoming a sect despised by Jew and Gentile Christian alike. It was therefore possible to allow traditional interpretations of prophetic scripture once again to be taught." (49:15)*

5. Genesis 12:2-3, 17:1, 5-6; 22:18 – Who Is the Seed of Abraham, Isaac and Jacob That Will Eventually Bless All the Nations?

The Biblical Text

"And Jehovah said to Abram, ...'I will make of you a great nation; I will bless you and make your name great, and you will be a blessing . . . and in you shall all families of the earth be blessed.'" (Genesis 12:2-3)

"[Almighty God says to Abram]: . . . For I have made you a father of many nations. And I will make you exceedingly fruitful, and I will make nations of you and kings shall come out of you." (Gen. 17:1, 5-6)

"[God states to Abraham]: And in your seed shall all the nations of the earth be blessed." (Gen. 22:18)

The Context of These Passages

In Genesis 12, God has commanded Abram to leave his own country and travel to "the land I will show you" (Gen. 12:1). There God promises He will make him into a "great nation" and that the entire earth will be blessed through him.

In Genesis 17, when Abram is ninety years old, the Lord appears to Abram and again tells him He will make him fruitful. God also tells him that nations and kings will come forth from his seed.

In Genesis 22, Abram (who is now Abraham because God changed his name) has been tested by God. Abraham showed God he is willing to do anything God asks. God sees this and promises Abraham that from *his seed* all the nations of the earth shall be blessed.

27

The Explanation of These Texts

Note here the repeated number of times God promises Abraham that all peoples on the earth will be blessed because of his seed.

It is likely that Abraham knew of the promise made by God to Adam and Eve that from the woman's seed a male descendant would come and crush Satan's head.

Now, God extends His promise through Abraham's seed. The question is, "Who is the offspring of Abraham God is speaking of who will bless all nations?"

At this point, it is too early to identify the person in the future who will bless all the nations. But whoever the specific person or seed will be, he *must* come from the seed of this one man, Abraham. Also, we must join God's promises to Eve with those He gave to Abraham. Thus, God's promised seed must not only be a man, but also a descendant of Abraham. As we will see, God further adds to the description of the promised seed, even while He continues to limit the line from which the special One will come: God next says He will come from the line of Abraham, then Isaac, and then Jacob.

Nevertheless, returning to this prophecy, we know from history that God blessed Abraham's seed both individually and collectively since: 1) God made Abraham into a great nation – the Jewish nation; 2) God did bless Abraham abundantly; 3) God did make his name great (He is honored by both Jews and Muslims). We also know that all peoples on the earth were blessed through Abraham, both culturally and spiritually.

> "In matters of banking and commerce and finance, the world owes Israel an immense debt. In matters of statesmanship, particularly international statesmanship, the debt is also large. From the time of David until now, Israelitish public men have been at the helm, sometimes in one nation and sometimes in another. In science and literature and music, the debt is likewise great. But high above all these things, the literature of Israel's

28

prophets has been translated into all languages. Israel has been made the channel for communicating to mankind the monotheism of the religion of Yahweh, ... Suppose we stop at this point, and ask: Has the promise been kept? Have all the families of the ground been blessed in Abraham and his seed? Who can answer otherwise than in the affirmative?'' (3:412-413)

But there is much more for us to consider. In the New Testament we discover that Jesus Christ was also a physical descendant of Abraham. The facts clearly show that no man has had such influence upon the world as Jesus Christ. (5:40-48)

The Apostle Matthew places at the front of his book this important statement: *"A record of the genealogy of Jesus Christ, the son of David, the son of Abraham"* (Mt. 1:1). Why? Because Matthew had read the Hebrew Scriptures and knew God had promised to bless all the nations through Abraham's seed. For Matthew, Jesus was the One God described to Abraham. The spiritual blessing of Abraham is also evident to the Apostle Paul who writes in Galatians 3:8: *"The Scripture foresaw that God would justify the Gentiles by faith [in Christ], and announced the gospel in advance to Abraham: 'All nations will be blessed through you [Abraham's seed].' So those who have faith are blessed along with Abraham, the man of faith."*

Because of space limitations, we cannot describe completely the increasingly narrow parental line God revealed, but a brief outline of the scriptural promises reveals that God's special Person could only come out of the following lineage and circumstances:

– from the seed of the woman (any possible man)

– from Abraham (one man's descendants are selected from all men on earth)

– from Isaac (not Ishmael: one half of Abraham's lineage is eliminated – Genesis 26:2-4)

– from Jacob (not Esau: one half of Jacob's lineage is now eliminated – Genesis 28:13-14)

29

– from Jesse (Isaiah 11:1; Luke 3:23, 32)

– from David (Jesse had at least eight sons; seven are now eliminated (1 Samuel 16:10-13)

– from Bethlehem (all cities in the world are now eliminated but one (Micah 5:2).

Clues to Identify the Messiah

Whoever the Messiah is, He *must* fit the following descriptions:

Clue #1 – He, a male child (the Hebrew text specifically uses a 3rd person, singular, masculine pronoun – "he"), will be born of the seed of the woman.

Clue #2 – He will come from the race of the Jews, and specifically from the seed of Abraham, Isaac and Jacob.

6. Deuteronomy 18:15 – Who Is the "Prophet Like Moses" of Whom God Says, "You Must Listen to Him"?

The Biblical Text

"[Moses is speaking] The Lord your God will raise up for you a prophet from among your own people, like myself; him you shall heed . . . . [God is speaking] I will raise up a prophet for them from among their own people, like yourself; I will put My words in his mouth and he will speak to them all that I command him; and if anybody fails to heed the words he speaks in My name, I Myself will call him to account.'' (Deuteronomy 18:15, 18, 19) – The Torah (97:1466)

The Context of the Passage

God, through Moses, is warning Israel to remain separate from the evil practices of the surrounding nations (Deut. 18:9-12). Included in His warning, God instructs Israel how to tell the difference between a "true prophet" and a "false prophet." Any prophet who speaks in the name of the Lord and his words do not come true is a "false prophet." God has not spoken through him. In the same context God tells Israel He will send prophets who will truthfully speak for Him. What's more, Israel can someday expect a prophet who will be "like Moses," that God will specially raise up.

The Explanation of the Text

Think for a moment. Would a "prophet like Moses" be a unique personage in Israel? Why would this "prophet like Moses" be considered a reference to the coming Messiah?

(1.) It is a fact that throughout its history, the nation of Israel did **not** apply to **any** prophet these particular words. That is not to say that one or two individual rabbis did not try to make the application to a favored prophet. But it cannot be denied that the nation of Israel as a whole never acknowledged any other prophet to be "like Moses." (52:II, 135-136)

(2.) This was not a reference to Joshua because (1) as we shall see there is no resemblance between Moses and Joshua; (2)

31

Joshua is never said to be a prophet nor does he fulfill the office of a prophet; (3) it was specifically stated in Joshua's own time *"no prophet has risen in Israel like Moses"* (Deut. 34:10).

(3.) The word "prophet" is in the singular, so it must refer to some individual prophet in the future.

(4.) Until Jesus came, no one was superior to Moses, for it was only said of Moses and Jesus that they knew the Lord and spoke to Him *"face to face"* (Deut. 34:10; cf. Num. 12:8; Mt. 3:17; Mk. 9:7; Jn. 11:41,42; 17:1-5, NIV).

(5.) Up to the time of Christ, it can be documented that the Jews had not believed that "the prophet" had yet arrived. Thus the leaders of Israel asked John the Baptist, *"Are you the prophet?"* (Jn. 1:21), which John denied. But, when the people saw Jesus' miracles, they said, *"Surely this is the Prophet who is to come into the world"* (Jn. 6:14).

What was the evidence that persuaded the people in Jesus' own time that He was the unique prophet God said was "like unto Moses"? Could anyone but the Messiah be worthy of being considered the One who is "like Moses"? The following parallels and contrasts will show that only Jesus completely fulfilled and went beyond Moses' prophetic office and is the unique One God promised would come.

A. *A great founder of religion*

Moses gave God's revelation of the law and founded the religion of Israel. Jesus gave God's complete revelation of grace and truth, fulfilled all the law and became the founder and Savior of the Christian religion (Jn. 1:17; Mt. 5:17; 1 Tim. 2:5-6).

B. *A great revealer of God*

Moses revealed God in writing the Torah. Moses did not point people to himself, but faithfully wrote about God and about the One in the future whom God told him about. Jesus claimed, *"For if you believed **Moses**, you would believe Me; **for he wrote of Me**. But if you do not believe His writings, how will you believe My words?"* (Jn. 5:46,47, NAS, emphasis added).

32

Jesus just didn't speak about God, but was God. He said, *"He who has seen Me has seen the Father . . . ."* (Jn. 14:6) and John said, *"No man has ever seen God [except] . . . the only unique Son, . . . He has revealed Him . . . ."* (Jn. 1:18, Amplified).

C. *A great Law-giver*

Moses was the only one authorized by God to give laws to Israel. It was Jesus who gave God's full understanding of the law and gave "new" laws to Israel. Jesus quoted the law when He said, *"You have heard that it was said . . . ,"* but added *what no other prophet had ever dared speak: "but I say unto you . . ."* (Mt. 5:21, 22). That's why *"when Jesus had finished teaching, the crowds were amazed at His teaching, because He taught as one who had authority, and not as their teachers of the law."* (Mt. 7:28,29, NIV)

D. *A great worker of miracles*

Moses was a great worker of miracles (the ten plagues on Egypt; the parting of the Red Sea, etc.) (Ex. 7-14; Deut. 34:10-12). But Jesus did greater works than Moses. He said, *"If I had not done among them [the miracles] what no one else did, they would not be guilty of sin; . . . ."* (Jn. 15:24, NIV).

In Acts we read, *"Men of Israel, listen to these words: Jesus the Nazarene, a man attested to you by God with miracles and wonders and signs which God performed through Him in your midst, just as you yourself know . . . ."* (Acts 2:22, NAS). Jesus commanded the elements, the wind and the water, raised the dead, gave sight to the blind, expelled the demons, and conquered death when He was resurrected from the dead (Mt. 8:23-27; 14:25; Lk. 7:11-15; 8:41,42; Jn. 9:1-7; Lk. 4:33-35; Jn. 2:19-22).

E. *A great Redeemer*

Moses rescued Israel from the bondage and slavery of Egypt (Ex. 3-4; Acts 7:20-39). Christ rescued the world from the bondage and slavery of sin (Eph. 2:1-8; Rom. 3:28-4:6).

F. *A great mediator*

Moses was the mediator between God and Israel. Jesus is the Mediator now between God and all humanity. 1 Timothy 2:5, 6 says, *"For there is one God and one mediator between God and men, the man Christ Jesus, who gave himself as a ransom for all men . . ."*

G. *A great intercessor*

Moses was the great intercessor for Israel, preventing God from utterly destroying them when they worshipped the golden calf (Ex. 32:7-14; Num. 14:11-22). Jesus is a greater intercessor. He now intercedes on behalf of all mankind (Jn. 3:16; Heb. 7:25; note Num. 21:4-9 and Jn. 3:14).

H. *A great prophet, judge and king*

Moses was a great prophet, judge and king (Ex. 18:13; Deut. 33:5). Jesus was a greater prophet, judge and king (Jn. 1:19-21, 29-34, 45; Mt. 2:2; Jn. 5:26-29; Heb. 7:17).

I. *Moses was like the Messiah; Jesus was the Messiah.*

"The woman said, 'I know that Messiah (called Christ) is coming. When he comes, he will explain everything to us.' Then Jesus declared, 'I who speak to you am He'" (Jn. 4:25, 26). He said, *"If you believed Moses, you would believe me, for he wrote about me"* (Jn. 5:46, NIV, emphasis added).

Was Deuteronomy 18:15 Recognized by the Jews as Messianic?

The Mishna, "Sefer ha-Mitzvot" in the Negative Commandments (13) states, *"The prophet whom God will raise up must be 'from among your own people'* (Deut. 18:15). This means also that He must arise in the land of Israel." (97:1472, 1766)

"The Talmud asserts 'that Messiah must be the greatest of future prophets, as being nearest in spirit to our master Moses.'" (52:II,114) "This prediction, then, could only receive its accomplishment in the Messiah. It was so understood by the Jews in the days of our Lord." (52:II,114)

Clues to Identify the Messiah

Whoever the Messiah is, He *must* fit the following descriptions:

Clue #1 – He, a male child (the Hebrew text specifically uses a 3rd person, singular, masculine pronoun – "he"), will be born of the seed of the woman.

Clue #2 – He will come from the race of the Jews, and specifically from the seed of Abraham, Isaac and Jacob.

Clue #3 – He will be a great prophet, with the authority to teach like Moses.

7. Psalm 22 – Who Is the One Crucified?

The Biblical Text

"My God, my God, why have you forsaken me . . . . All who see me mock me; they hurl insults, shaking their heads: he trusts in the Lord; let the Lord rescue him. Let him deliver him, since he delights in him . . . . I am poured out like water, and all of my bones are out of joint. My heart has turned to wax; it has melted away within me. My strength is dried up like a potsherd, and my tongue sticks to the roof of my mouth; you lay me in the dust of death. Dogs have surrounded me; a band of evil men has encircled me, they have pierced my hands and my feet. I can count all my bones; people stare and gloat over me. They divide my garments among them and cast lots for my clothing" (Ps. 22:1, 7-8, 14-18, NIV).

The Context of the Passage

Psalm 22 is both a cry of anguish and a song of praise to God. The NIV Bible properly identifies the context of this passage as "the anguished prayer of David as a godly sufferer victimized by the vicious and prolonged attacks of enemies whom he has not provoked and from whom the Lord has not (yet) delivered him." (98:805)

The Hebrew scholar Charles Briggs states in his book, ***Messianic Prophecy***: "Psalm 22 describes a sufferer with stretched body, feverish frame and pierced hands and feet. He is surrounded by cruel enemies, who mock him for his trust in God, and divide his garments as their spoil. He is abandoned by God for a season, until he is brought to the dust of death. He is then delivered, and praises his deliverer with sacrifices." (51:323)

The Explanation of the Text

In this passage that describes the feelings and circumstances of David, we find astonishing parallels that fit the future experience of Jesus Christ on the cross. The question is: "Are these parallels

36

fiction, found only in the minds of Christians or words that David wrote a thousand years before Christ which perfectly fit the person of Jesus Christ?''

As Baron has observed: "Are Christians right in interpreting this Psalm as a prediction of Christ? . . . It is the only interpretation which accords with common sense.'' (55:263) The following is an explanation of the actual words in the Psalm and a look at the incredibly accurate picture they paint of Jesus Christ during His crucifixion *one thousand years later*.

> 1. David said, *"My God, my God, why have you forsaken me?"* (Ps. 22:1).

Jesus said these exact words while dying on the cross (Mt. 27:46). They accurately expressed His grief as He bore our sins (1 Pet. 2:24). Having the sins of all humanity placed to His account resulted in His separation from God, His Father (Gal. 3:13-14).

> 2. David said, *"All who see me mock me. They hurl insults, shaking their heads"* (Ps. 22:7). The meaning of the word "shake" is "to shake or wag the head in mockery." (95:631) It is also a gesture of scorn and includes the fact that the adversaries were not only giving assent and approval to the victim's suffering, but also enjoyed seeing his adversities and calamities. (76:385, 386)

Jesus was literally scorned, despised and mocked by the crowds surrounding Him on the cross. The words David used, *"They hurl insults, shaking their heads,"* perfectly fit: 1) the religious rulers who stood watching (*"the rulers even sneered at Him"* – Lk. 23:35); 2) the soldiers (*"the soldiers also came up and mocked Him"* – Lk. 23:36-38); and 3) one of the two criminals crucified next to Him (*"one of the criminals who hung there hurled insults at Him: 'Aren't you the Christ [Messiah]?'''* – Lk. 23:39). Herod and his soldiers (leading up to His crucifixion) also mocked Him (*"then Herod and his soldiers ridiculed and mocked him"* – Lk. 23:11). At His trials the chief priests and the teachers of the law did the same (*"the chief priests and the teachers of the law were standing there, vehemently accusing him"* – Lk. 23:10). Finally, Matthew records

37

(about the crowd), *"Those who passed by hurled insults at him, shaking their heads . . . 'Come down from the cross if you are the Son of God'"* – Mt. 27:39, 40).

> 3. David reveals that his enemies mocked and insulted Him by saying, *"He trusts in the Lord; let the Lord rescue him. Let him deliver him, since he delights in him"* (Ps. 22:8).

Jesus' enemies used the words David wrote one thousand years earlier to hurl their insults at Christ on the cross. They said, *"He trusts in God. Let God rescue him now if he wants him"* (Mt. 27:43).

> 4. David said, *"I am poured out like water and all my bones are out of joint. My heart is turned to wax. It is melted within me. My strength is dried up like a potsherd . . . ."* (Ps. 22:14, 15)

Like water, Jesus' blood on the cross "poured out" of His body. Also, it is a fact that crucifixion pulls the bones and the body out of joint. This is what happened to Jesus.

When "blood *and* water" came forth from Jesus' pierced side (Jn. 19:34), this was medical proof that His heart had literally burst, fulfilling David's words, *"My heart has turned to wax. It has melted away within me"* (Ps. 22:14). (33:199; 96:129-147)

Finally, Jesus' strength dried up. He thirsted and then He died (Ps. 22:15; Jn. 19:28-30).

> 5. David said, *"Dogs have surrounded me; a band of evil men has encircled me, they have pierced my hands and my feet"* (Ps. 22:16).

Jesus was encircled by people who hated Him, mocked Him and were glad to watch Him suffer and die. They pierced His hands and His feet when they nailed Him to the cross just as David said (Jn. 19:15-18).

> 6. David said, *"I can count all my bones; people stare and gloat over me. They divide my garments among them and cast lots for my clothing"* (Ps. 22:17, 18).

38

Jesus, while dying on the cross, looked down on the soldiers who had crucified Him and watched them gamble for His garments. For those who state that Jesus and the Gospel writers planned and acted out the prophecies of David, they must answer how Jesus motivated and arranged for the soldiers to gamble for His garments.

Also, how did He keep the soldiers from breaking His bones, a common Roman practice? Amazingly, Jesus was the only one of the three who were crucified whose legs were not broken (see Ps. 34:20). He was also the only one who suffered an unusual spear thrust into His side (fulfilling Zech. 12:10) that also did not break a bone (Jn. 19:31-37).

The Apostle John watched the entire crucifixion. Afterwards, as he thought back on what he had seen and thought about what was said in the Psalms, Isaiah and Zechariah, he realized all of them had specifically said the Messiah would be pierced. As we shall see, Zechariah even prophesies, *"They will look on me [Jehovah God] the One they have pierced"* (Zech. 12:10). (See also Isaiah 53:5 and John 19:34).

Was Psalm 22 Recognized by the Jews as Messianic?

Few rabbis have accepted this passage as Messianic because of the dislike for a *suffering* and *crucified* Messiah. But the rabbinical writing called the *Pesikta Rabbat* (Piska 36:1-2), compiled in the ninth century A.D. at the latest, although from much earlier material, refers to part of this passage as having reference to certain persons' sins that will weight Messiah down under a yoke of iron. Thus, it says, "The Messiah's body is bent low" with great suffering (13:74).

In addition, the great Hebrew scholar Edersheim observes that a remarkable comment appears in Yalkut* on Isaiah 60 which applies this passage in Psalm 22 to the Messiah, and uses almost the same words as the Gospel evangelists who describe the mocking behavior of the crowds surrounding the cross. (47:II,718)

As the late professor Charles Briggs of Union Theological Seminary, the man whose name appears on the official Hebrew Lexicon of the Hebrew Scriptures, stated (95):

"These sufferings [of Ps. 22] transcend those of any historical sufferer, with the single exception of Jesus Christ. They find their exact counterpart in the sufferings of the cross . . . . This ideal is a Messianic ideal, and finds its only historical realization in Jesus Christ." (51:326, 327)

But most Jewish people have rejected the idea of a suffering Messiah, in spite of this passage and Isaiah 53 (see below). For example, David Baron, who had a strict rabbinical education, dismissed as completely absurd the idea that the Messiah would suffer. But the Hebrew Scriptures taught him the absolute need for forgiveness of sins (74:38-39) and brought him to the conclusion that the Scriptures did predict the Messiah would suffer for our sins. This led him to accept Jesus as the Messiah because "Jesus of Nazareth is the only individual in the [entire] history of the Jewish nation in whom all these [prophetic] characteristics are to be found." (55:265)

Yalkut is the name given to the well known collection of many older, accredited explanations and interpretations of the Hebrew testament.

Clues to Identify the Messiah

Whoever the Messiah is, He **must** fit the following descriptions:

Clue #1 – He, a male child (the Hebrew text specifically uses a 3rd person, singular, masculine pronoun – "he"), will be born of the seed of the woman.

Clue #2 – He will come from the race of the Jews, and specifically from the seed of Abraham, Isaac and Jacob.

Clue #3 – He will be a great prophet, with the authority to teach like Moses.

Clue #4 – He will be mocked, and people will cast lots for His garments while He suffers.

8. Psalm 110:1 – Who Is David's "Lord"?

The Biblical Text

"The Lord says to my Lord, 'Sit at my right hand until I make your enemies a footstool for your feet.'" (Psalm 110:1)

The Context of the Passage

In this psalm Jehovah God makes a declaration addressed to one called, "My Lord." This cannot be David. This must be the Messiah. Why?

In 2 Samuel 7:16, God promises David, *"Your house and your kingdom **will endure forever** before me; your throne will be established forever."* (Emphasis added.) David replied, *"O sovereign Lord, you have also spoken about **the future** of the house of your servant"* (2 Sam. 7:19, emphasis added).

God's promise that He would establish an everlasting kingdom and that David's house would last forever became the focal point for many later prophecies. Who would be the great King whose throne would last forever? Whoever he would be, he would not only be a male (out of the seed of Eve; remember the third person singular, masculine pronoun "he" found in Genesis 3:15?), but also from the line of Abraham, Isaac, Jacob and now David.

With this in mind, in this Psalm, David records, *"Jehovah says to my Lord (my sovereign, therefore superior to David), 'Sit at my right hand.'"* Since God is stating this, the one addressed would have the high place of honor next to God.

This is evidence that the One described is the coming Messiah. It is only the Messiah whose kingdom and throne will be established forever (according to 2 Samuel 7:16). Only the Messiah can be the future son of David who is "anointed" by God as the eternal King-Priest in Jerusalem after the order of Melchizedek. *"The Lord has sworn and will not change his mind: You are a priest forever, in the order of Melchizedek."* Then David states once more that *"the Lord is at your [God's] right hand"* (Ps. 110:4, 5; cf. Heb. 7:11-24).

Even though David and Solomon did lead worship-related activities, such as building and overseeing the temple, overseeing the work of the priests and Levites and the temple liturgy, they were not permitted to engage in those specifically priestly functions that had been assigned to the priesthood (see 2 Chronicles 26:16-18). (98:907)

Therefore Psalm 110 cannot refer to King David or Solomon or any of their royal descendants (other than the Messiah). Only David's "Lord" will sit at God's right hand, and will be an eternal priest in the order of Melchizedek. Nowhere does Scripture mention that David or Solomon sat at God's right hand or that they were eternal priests. Therefore this could only refer to the Messiah.

The Explanation of the Text

Whom is this Psalm about? How can it be explained? One person in history presented such a forceful explanation that the leaders in Israel who heard it couldn't think of any way to refute it.

The teacher who explained this psalm to the leaders in Israel was none other than Jesus Christ. Listen to His articulate explanation of this passage and see if you can argue with Him.

"While the Pharisees were gathered together, Jesus asked them, 'What do you think about the Christ [Messiah]? Whose son is he?' 'The son of David,' they replied. He said to them, 'How is it then that David, speaking by the Spirit, calls him "Lord"? For he says, "The Lord said to my Lord: 'Sit at my right hand until I put your enemies under your feet.'"' If then David calls him "Lord," how can he be his son?' No one could say a word in reply, and from that day on no one dared to ask him any more questions." (Mt. 22:41-45, NIV; cf. Acts 2:34-36; Heb. 1:13; 5:6-10; 7:11-28)

Here Jesus argues the text says, 1) the Messiah was a descendant of David (the Pharisees agreed); 2) the Messiah will be more than a descendant of David – He will be David's Lord. Jesus' question, *"If David then calls him 'Lord' how can he be his son?,"* presented a dilemma to the scribes and Pharisees who did not believe Jesus was the Messiah.

Jesus could prove to them He was descended from the lineage of David. If He could show the Pharisees that according to this passage in the Psalms David was addressing someone superior to him who would be given the high place of honor next to God and would *also* be one of his descendants, then Jesus' claims to be God and the Messiah would be in line with Scripture.

Repeatedly, the historical accounts of Jesus' life showed that the Pharisees attempted to stone Jesus for His statements of being God (see below).

The dilemma faced by the religious leaders of Israel is the same one facing us today. How can we escape the logic of Jesus' argument that the One described as "my Lord" in Psalm 110 could be none other than Jesus Himself, who was a descendant of David? Who else fits the description of being David's Lord? Who else would claim the high position next to God? Who else could be the Mediator and Priest along the line of Melchizedek? Who else came and gave His life a ransom for the many? There is no one else but Jesus Christ.

In Psalm 110 we are told that the Messiah is to be far more than a mere man. He will sit at God's right hand. This is a position of privilege and authority given to no one else, human or angel, in the entire Hebrew Scripture. In addition, this One is called "Lord" and will be an eternal priest (Ps. 110:1, 4).

If so, this One will be *simultaneously* a prophet (Deut. 18:15), eternal priest (Ps. 110:4) and king (Gen. 49:10). But no one in the entire history of the Hebrew nation has ever claimed to be such a One – except Jesus. What is even more amazing is that in the verses to come we will see that the Messiah was to be the eternal One Himself – God. And no prophet, priest or king in all of Israel's history, has ever claimed to be God.

Jesus told the scribes and Pharisees that He eternally existed before Abraham was born: *"Truly, truly I say to you, before Abraham was born I AM [Gk. ego eimi, i.e., eternally existed]"* (Jn. 8:58).

Jesus also claimed He was one in nature or essence with God: *"I and the Father are one [Gk. one in essence]"* (Jn. 10:30). The

43

religious leaders were angry with Him because *"He was calling God his [very] own Father, making himself equal with God"* (Jn. 5:18).

In fact, on three different occasions the religious leaders tried to stone Jesus to death because they realized the implications of what He was saying. They reported He was openly claiming that He was God Himself. The New Testament specifically records they were attempting to stone Him *"because you, being a man, make yourself out to be God"* (Jn. 10:33; 5:18).

What does this mean? It means that Jesus fits the portrait given of the Messiah in the Hebrew Scriptures. (In our next verse, we will prove the Messiah was to be both God and man.)

Was Psalm 110 Recognized by the Jews as Messianic?

In his appendix documenting rabbinic interpretations of Messianic passages, Edersheim states of Psalm 110 that it " . . . .is throughout applied to the Messiah. To begin with, it evidently underlines the Targumic rendering of verse 4 . . . . In the Midrash on Psalm xviii.36 . . . , Psalm cx. [110], verse 1, 'Sit thou at my right hand' is specifically applied to the Messiah, ..." (47:II,720-721)

This text was acknowledged as Messianic by Jewish rabbis before the time of Christ. Keil and Delitzsch have concluded that by its very usage in the New Testament, the Messianic nature of Psalm 110 had to be understood by the scribes and Pharisees at the time of Christ. (90:184-185)

In addition, noted theologian and biblical scholar J. P. Lange observes that because of the very words in the text, "the Messianic interpretation is demanded" and that the psalm was generally understood as Messianic – "Thus, did the Synagogue understand it in earlier times [before the Christian era]." (91:554-555)

Also, the NIV Study Bible which represents the best of modern conservative scholarship comments, "Before the Christian era Jews already viewed it as Messianic." (98:906)

Clues to Identify the Messiah

Whoever the Messiah is, He *must* fit the following descriptions:

Clue #1 – He, a male child (the Hebrew text specifically uses a 3rd person, singular, masculine pronoun – "he"), will be born of the seed of the woman.

Clue #2 – He will come from the race of the Jews, and specifically from the seed of Abraham, Isaac and Jacob.

Clue #3 – He will be a great prophet, with the authority to teach like Moses.

Clue #4 – He will be mocked, and people will cast lots for His garments while He suffers.

Clue #5 – He will be David's Lord.

9. Isaiah 9:6-7 – Who Is the Child That Is God and Will Have an Everlasting Kingdom?

The Biblical Text

"For to us a child is born, to us a son is given, and the government will be on his shoulders. And he will be called Wonderful Counselor, Mighty God, Everlasting Father, Prince of Peace. Of the increase of his government and peace there will be no end. He will reign on David's throne and over his kingdom, establishing and upholding it with justice and righteousness from that time on and forever. The zeal of the Lord Almighty will accomplish this." (Isaiah 9:6-7)

The Context of the Passage

Israel has been invaded by the Assyrian King Tiglath-Pileser (the first Jewish captivity). The captured Israelites are plunged into despair and humiliation.

In this prophecy God offers them hope for the future. God speaks of a coming Light who will illuminate those who are in distress, gloom and darkness – *"the people walking in darkness have seen a great light; on those living in the land of the shadow of death a light has dawned"* (Isa. 9:2).

Isaiah the Prophet records that in the past God had humbled the land of Zebulun and the land of Naphtali (Northern and Southern Galilee). However, in the future God *"will honor Galilee . . ."* (Isa. 9:1). It is these people who, walking in darkness, will "see a great light."

Then God proceeds to describe the child born, the Son given, who will be both a human, and God, and who will reign forever on David's throne. This can be no other than the promised Messiah.

The Explanation of the Text

What this prophecy makes clear is the following:

    1. A child will be born to the Jewish people.

2. The government will be upon His shoulders –
   He will be a ruling King.

3. He is called "Wonderful Counselor," "Mighty
   God," "Everlasting Father," "Prince of
   Peace" – as Dr. Merrill Unger points out, the
   phrase "his name" is a Hebrew idiom, and
   means that the child would not actually bear
   the names, but "deserve them, and that they
   are appellatives or descriptive designations of
   his person and work." (41:1167-1168)

4. There would be no end to the increase of the
   child's government and peace.

5. He would reign on David's throne and over his
   kingdom forever and ever.

6. The zeal of God Almighty would accomplish
   it.

7. The passage places the fulfillment of this
   prophecy in Galilee as God says He will honor
   *Galilee of the Gentiles, by way of the sea,
   along the Jordan."*

Concerning Zebulun and Naphtali, Hebrew scholar Edward J.
Young comments, "Zebulun and Naphtali, the two north-eastern
tribes of the land west of the Jordan (later known as upper and lower
Galilee) were first devastated and depopulated by Tiglath-Pileser
. . . (2 Kgs. 15:29) . . . This despised district, despised even in
New Testament times, was glorified when God honored it, and the
fulfillment of the prophecy occurred when Jesus Christ the Son of
God dwelt [settled] in Capernaum ['*in the region of Zebulun and
Naphtali*' – Mt. 4:13]." (58:323-324)

In Psalm 110:1 we saw the first biblical reference that stated the
Messiah would sit at God's right hand and therefore would be
second only to God Himself. Here in Isaiah 9:6 we have the clearest
statement that the Messiah will be both God and man: He is called
"Eternal Father" and "Mighty God," (El Gibbor) – the name used
of God Himself in Isaiah 10:21.

47

Some scholars have written, "The Messiah early became known not only as the son of David but also as the Son of God. *'Thou art my Son, this day have I begotten thee'* (Ps. 2:7b) . . . ." (58:330)

Young has shown that the use of *El* in Isaiah "is found as a designation of God and only of him . . . .[thus we see that] the Lord, the Holy One of Israel – and *El Gibbor* [the term used of the Son in Isaiah 9:6], are one and the same." (58:336)

So, for our purposes, what is most important to realize in this prophecy is that God says the Messiah will be *both* God and man. If so, no one else in human history has claimed 1) to be God, 2) to be the Messiah and 3) proved it by rising from the dead, except Jesus Christ. (68; 69; 70).

Was Isaiah 9:6-7 Recognized by the Jews as Messianic?

There can be no doubt that Jewish rabbis have accepted these verses as clearly applying to the Messiah.

The Targum of Isaiah rendered this passage, "His name has been called from of old, Wonderful Counselor, Mighty God, He who lives forever, the Anointed One (or Messiah), in whose days peace shall increase upon us." (73:32)

Theologian and professor of biblical criticism at the University of Aberdeen Paton J. Gloag observed that, "The ancient Jews refer these words *only* to the Messiah. 'The prophet,' says the Targum of Jonathan, 'speaketh of the house of David, because a child is born to us, a son is given to us, . . . his name is called of old Wonderful in counsel, God the mighty, He who abideth forever, *the Messiah* whose peace shall be abundant upon us in His days.'" (52, II:115, emphasis added; cf. 47:723)

Clues to Identify the Messiah

Whoever the Messiah is, He *must* fit the following descriptions:

Clue #1 – He, a male child (the Hebrew text specifically uses a 3rd person, singular, masculine pronoun – "he"), will be born of the seed of the woman.

Clue #2 – He will come from the race of the Jews, and specifically from the seed of Abraham, Isaac and Jacob.

Clue #3 – He will be a great prophet, with the authority to teach like Moses.

Clue #4 – He will be mocked, and people will cast lots for His garments while He suffers.

Clue #5 – He will be David's Lord.

Clue #6 – He will be the child born who is God, and will have an everlasting kingdom.

10. Isaiah 53 – Who Was Crushed and Pierced for Our Transgressions So That We Would Be Healed by His Wounds; upon Whom Did the Lord Lay the Iniquity of All Mankind?

The Biblical Text

"Who has believed our message and to whom has the arm of the Lord been revealed? He grew up before him like a tender shoot, and like a root out of dry ground. He had no beauty or majesty to attract us to him, nothing in his appearance that we should desire him. He was despised and rejected by men, a man of sorrows, and familiar with suffering. Like one from whom men hide their faces he was despised, and we esteemed him not. Surely he took up our infirmities and carried our sorrows, yet we considered him stricken by God, smitten by him, and afflicted. But he was pierced for our transgressions, he was crushed for our iniquities; the punishment that brought us peace was upon him, and by his wounds we are healed. We all, like sheep, have gone astray, each of us has turned to his own way; and the Lord has laid on him the iniquity of us all. He was oppressed and afflicted, yet he did not open his mouth; he was led like a lamb to the slaughter, and as a sheep before her shearers is silent, so he did not open his mouth. By oppression and judgment he was taken away. And who can speak of his descendants? For he was cut off from the land of the living; for the transgression of my people he was stricken. He was assigned a grave with the wicked, and with the rich in his death, though he had done no violence, nor was any deceit in his mouth. Yet it was the Lord's will to crush him and cause him to suffer, and though the Lord makes his life a guilt offering, he will see his offspring and prolong his days, and the will of the Lord will prosper in his hand. After

50

the suffering of his soul, he will see the light of life and be satisfied; by his knowledge my righteous servant will justify many, and he will bear their iniquities. Therefore I will give him a portion among the great, and he will divide the spoils with the strong, because he poured out his life unto death, and was numbered with the transgressors. For he bore the sin of many, and made intercession for the transgressors.'' (Isaiah 53:1-12)

The Context of the Passage

This passage is about the "Servant of the Lord." We find that the "Servant of the Lord" is a future individual Isaiah describes in what are called his "Servant Song" passages. Most agree that the passages devoted to describing the Servant are: Isaiah 42:1-7; 49:1-7; 50:4-10; and 52:13-53:12.

In these passages, we discover "the Servant" is the Messiah. What evidence proves this?

The texts themselves prove this, for "the Servant" is *"the chosen One in whom Jehovah delights''* (Isa. 42:1), His mission is to bring the nation of Israel back to Jehovah (Isa. 49:5), and He is to be *"a light to the gentiles''* – in other words, to all the nations of the earth (Isa. 42:1,6). This is not Israel because "the Servant" *"has not been rebellious''* (Isa. 50:5).

Isaiah 52:13-53:12 is the fourth and longest of the four Servant passages. Significantly, the passage is quoted and applied to Jesus Christ more frequently by New Testament writers than any other passage in the Hebrew Scriptures.

In the text itself, Jehovah God calls this individual *"My Servant''* (Isa. 52:13), and states His Servant will ultimately be successful: *"He will be raised and lifted up and greatly exalted''* (Isa. 52:13). In the Hebrew these are the *same* words used by Isaiah to describe the Lord (Jehovah of Hosts) in Isaiah 6:1, 3.

But in verses 14 and 15, it doesn't look as if the Servant is successful. At the first appearance of the Servant, God informs us,

"Many will be appalled at him" since His appearance is disfigured, marred, and almost beyond human likeness (Isa. 53:14). But then, very mysteriously and quickly, the picture changes. The text says, *"**Just as there were many** who were appalled at him [the first picture], **so will many** nations shut their mouths at Him"* the next time they see Him (Isa. 53:15, emphasis added).

Could verse 14 be referring to Jesus Christ's first coming, when He is smitten, bruised, and beaten? Could verse 15 be His second coming when He will return as the triumphant Messiah who rules in power?

As Dr. Walter Kaiser has correctly pointed out, according to the text, "men would reject the Servant's message (53:1), His person (verse 2), and His mission (verse 3). But His vicarious suffering would effect an atonement between God and man (verses 4-6); and though He would submit to suffering (verse 7), death (verse 8), and burial (verse 9), He would subsequently be raised to life, exalted and richly rewarded (verses 10-12)." (30:217)

Who could Isaiah's Servant be? Who else but Jesus Christ ever claimed He was the Messiah (Mt. 26:63-65; Jn. 4:25,26), claimed His blood was poured out for many for the forgiveness of sins (Mt. 26:28, cf. Isa. 53:12), and rose again from the grave (Lk. 24:45,46, cf. Isa. 53:10,11) to validate His claims?

The Explanation of the Text

Does this chapter really refer to the Person of the Messiah? Even though Isaiah writes that the Servant was personally chosen by Jehovah (Isa. 42:1), and was given the mission of bringing the nation of Israel back to God (Isa. 49:5), there are some who still believe this passage does *not* refer to the Messiah.

Rather, they think that the Servant who suffers in Isaiah 52 and 53 is actually Isaiah the Prophet himself. They say Isaiah is using "figurative language" just like Jeremiah who said, *"I am like a sheep led to the slaughter"* (Jer. 11:19). Everybody knows Jeremiah wasn't a sheep nor was he literally led to the slaughter. Therefore, like Jeremiah, Isaiah is only speaking poetically to describe his sufferings.

Further, they claim that even in Jesus' own day we find an Ethiopian eunuch reading Isaiah 53. He asks Philip, *"Tell me, of whom does the prophet speak? Of himself, or of somebody else?"* (Acts 8:30-35) Some surmise the eunuch might have learned this interpretation from some of the Jerusalem rabbis. Regardless, this was, and still is considered a possible interpretation by many people.

A second interpretation is that the suffering Servant stands for the nation of Israel. Israel has suffered greatly throughout history and possibly Isaiah figuratively speaks of the nation as the expiatory lamb for mankind. Some think Isaiah is saying that God has placed upon Israel the full impact of all mankind's sins so that all humanity can survive. (56:22)

But there are reasons why these two interpretations should be rejected.

First, the biblical text itself teaches us the suffering Servant could *not* be Isaiah or the nation of Israel. The reason for this is found in verses 9 and 10 where we are told the Servant *"had done no violence, nor was any deceit found in his mouth."* This couldn't be Isaiah or the nation since Isaiah himself clearly states, *"I am a man of unclean lips, and I live among a people of unclean lips"* (Isa. 6:5, emphasis added).

In another place Isaiah confesses, *"Our offenses are many in your sight, and our sins testify against us"* (Isa. 59:12, NIV). So the biblical text itself proves neither Isaiah nor Israel fits the description of the suffering Servant who had *"done no violence, nor was any deceit found in his mouth"* (v. 9).

There is another reason why this passage must be a description of the coming Messiah and *cannot* be referring to either Isaiah or the nation of Israel. That reason is found in verse 10. There we learn, the suffering Servant gives his life as a "guilt offering," a "trespass offering."

According to the Hebrew Scriptures, a trespass offering *must be* a lamb without blemish; it *must be* perfect (Lev. 6:6, 7). The life

53

that's given must be a perfect life. Here again, Isaiah the Prophet admits neither he nor the nation of Israel qualifies. They are not perfect, rather, they are both guilty of sin.

Finally, proof that Isaiah is speaking of the coming Messiah and not the nation of Israel is found in 53:8 where the text states, *"For the transgression of My people, he was stricken."* Who are the "my people" spoken about? This must be Israel. But, if the "Servant" is stricken for the transgression of "My people," then the servant can't be Israel. This must be the Messiah who will suffer.

Throughout this passage, the Servant is portrayed as an individual. It speaks of what *He* has done; how *He* was despised; how *He* was rejected, and how the Lord laid on Him the iniquity of us all. All of this the Servant did on behalf of "My people."

Is This Text Speaking of Jesus Christ?

(1) *"But he was pierced for our transgressions"* (53:5).
 • *"And when they came to the place called the skull, there they crucified him . . ."* (Lk. 23:33).
 • *"Jesus, while on the cross, was pierced in His side by a soldier's spear, bringing a sudden flow of blood and water"* (Jn. 19:34).

(2) *"He was crushed for our iniquities; the punishment that brought us peace was upon him and by his wounds we are healed"* (53:5).
 • *"And he himself bore our sins in his body on the cross, that we might die to sin and live to righteousness; for by his wounds you were healed"* (1 Pet. 2:24).

(3) *"We all, like sheep, have gone astray, each of us has turned to his own way; and the Lord has laid on him the iniquity of us all"* (53:6).
 • *"God was in Christ reconciling the world to himself, not counting their trespasses against them, . . ."* (2 Cor. 5:19).
 • Peter said about Jesus' death on the cross, *"For Christ died for our sins once for all, the righteous for the unrighteous, to bring you to God"* (1 Pet. 3:18); *". . . for you were like sheep going astray, . . ."* (1 Pet. 2:25).

(4) *"He was oppressed and afflicted, yet he did not open his mouth. He was led like a lamb to the slaughter, and as a sheep*

before his shearers is silent, so he did not open his mouth'' (53:8).

- *"When he was accused by the chief priests and the elders, he gave no answer. Then Pilate asked him, 'Don't you hear the testimony they are bringing against you?' But Jesus made no reply, not even to a single charge – to the great amazement of the governor''* (Mt. 27:12-14).

(5) *"By oppression and judgment he was taken away''* (53:8).

- *" 'Am I leading a rebellion,' said Jesus, 'that you have come out with swords and clubs to capture me? Every day I was with you, teaching in the temple courts, and you did not arrest me. But the scripture must be fulfilled.' Then everyone deserted him and fled . . . The chief priests and the whole Sanhedran were looking for evidence against Jesus so that they could put him to death, but they did not find any. Many testified falsely against him, but their statements did not agree . . . They all condemned him as worthy of death. Then some began to spit at him; they blindfolded him, struck him with their fists, and said, 'Prophesy!' And the guards took him and beat him''* (Mk. 14:48-50, 55, 56, 64, 65).

(6) *"For he was cut off from the land of the living, for the trangression of my people he was stricken''* (53:8).

- *"But you disowned the Holy and Righteous One . . . and put to death the Prince of Life . . . For you first, God raised up his Servant . . .''* (Acts 3:14-15, 26).

- *"For while we were still helpless, at the right time Christ died for the ungodly . . . . God demonstrates his own love toward us, in that while we were yet sinners, Christ died for us''* (Rom. 5:6, 8).

(7) *"He was assigned a grave with the wicked, and with the rich in his death, though he had done no violence, nor was any deceit in his mouth''* (53:9).

- *"So as evening approached, Joseph of Arimathea, a prominent member of the Council, who was himself waiting for the kingdom of God, went boldly to Pilate and asked for Jesus' body. Pilate was surprised to hear that he was already dead. Summoning the centurion, he asked him if Jesus had already died. When he learned from the centurion that it was so, he gave the body to Joseph. So Joseph bought some linen cloth,* took down the body, wrapped it in the linen, and placed it in a tomb cut out of rock. Then he rolled a stone against the entrance of the tomb" (Mk. 15:42-46).

(8) *"Yet it was the Lord's will to crush him and cause him to suffer, and though the Lord makes his life a guilt offering, . . ."* (Isa. 53:10).

- *"But the things which God announced beforehand by the mouth of all the prophets, that his Christ [Messiah] should suffer he has thus fulfilled"* (Acts 3:18).
- *"All this is from God . . . God was reconciling the world to himself in Christ . . ."* (2 Cor. 5:18, 19).

(9) *"After the suffering of his soul, he will see the light of life and be satisfied. By his knowledge my righteous servant will justify many, and he will bear their iniquities"* (Isa. 53:11).

- *"For I delivered to you as of first importance what I also received, that Christ died for our sins according to the scriptures, and that he was buried, and that he was raised on the third day according to the scriptures, and that he appeared to Cephas, then to the twelve. After that he appeared to more than five hundred brethren at one time, . . ."* (1 Cor. 15:3-6).
- *". . . being justified as a gift by his grace through the redemption which is in Christ Jesus; . . ."* (Rom. 3:24).

(10) *". . .Because he poured out his life unto death, and was numbered with the transgressors. For he bore the sin of many, and made intercession for the transgressors"* (Isa. 53:12).

- *"Two robbers were crucified with him, one on his right and one on his left"* (Mt. 27:38).
- *". . . Father, forgive them, for they do not know what they are doing . . ."* (Lk. 23:34).
- *"He was delivered over to death for our sins and was raised to life for our justification"* (Rom. 4:25).
- *"Christ Jesus, who died – more than that, who was raised to life – is at the right hand of God and is also interceding for us"* (Rom. 8:34).
- *"Therefore he is able to save completely those who come to God through him, because he always lives to intercede for them"* (Heb. 7:25).

As the Scottish exegete and theologian Paton J. Gloag, former professor of biblical criticism at the University of Aberdeen, argues:

> "We do not see how anyone can read this remarkable prophecy without being struck with its pointed resemblance to the character, sufferings, and death of the Lord Jesus. The portrait is complete: the resemblance is striking and unmistakable. Indeed, it seems more like a history of the past than a prediction of the future: A statement of the doctrines of the gospel made by some New Testament writer, as Saint Paul or Saint John, rather than a prediction of some Old Testament prophet. The seven centuries which intervened between Isaiah and Christ seemed to be bridged over, and the future is painted in the characters of the present. In no portion of Scripture, even in the most Evangelical parts of the New Testament, is the doctrine of the atonement, that grand characteristic of Christianity, so clearly stated as in these words of the prophet: 'Surely he hath borne our griefs, and carried our sorrows; he was wounded for our transgressions, he was bruised for our iniquities: the chastisement of our peace was upon him, and with his stripes we are healed. The Lord hath laid upon him the iniquity of us all.' And yet nothing is more indisputable than that these words were uttered centuries before our Lord came into this world." (52:II,286-287)

Was Isaiah 52:13-Isaiah 53 Recognized by the Jews as Messianic?

Proof that this passage has long been acknowledged as Messianic can be seen from the fact that the early rabbis developed the idea of two Messiahs from this passage. Why?

First, they could not reconcile the statements that so clearly spoke of a suffering and dying Messiah with those verses in other passages that spoke of a triumphant and victorious Messiah. What is important to note is that they did recognize that both pictures somehow applied to the Messiah. But they also assumed it was impossible to reconcile both views in one person.

Rather than seeing one Messiah in two different roles, they saw two Messiahs – the suffering and dying Messiah, called "Messiah ben Joseph," and the victorious conquering Messiah, called "Messiah ben David."

Today, some Orthodox Jews still wait for the political Messiah, who will conquer and rule forever. At the same time there are some who accept Jesus Christ as the "other" Messiah (Messiah ben Joseph) although they deny His Deity. (94:6)

Dr. Raphael Patai, formerly of the University of Jerusalem, who has authored 20 books on subjects relating to Jewish religious beliefs, has stated, "When the death of the Messiah became an established tenet in Talmudic times, this was felt to be irreconcilable with the belief in the Messiah as the Redeemer who would usher in the blissful millennium of the Messianic age. The dilemma was solved by splitting the person of the Messiah in two . . . ." (14:166) On the basis of Isaiah 53, the Babylonian Talmud boldly predicts, "Messiah ben Joseph will be slain . . . ." (14:167)

The different views that orthodox rabbis down through history have given to this passage can be found in *Rays of Messiah's Glory*. Notice, even such rabbis as the great Maimonides and Rabbi Crispin thought it was wrong to apply Isaiah 53 to the nation of Israel. Rather, they thought this clearly described God's Messiah:

> ". . . the weight of Jewish authority preponderates in favor of the Messianic interpretation of this chapter; . . . . That until recent times this prophecy has been almost universally received by Jews as referring to Messiah is evident from Targum [J]onathan, who introduces Messiah by name in chapter LII.13; from the Talmud ('Sanhedran,' fol. 98, b); and from the Zohar, ... In fact, until Rashi [Rabbi Solomon Izaaki (1040-1105), considered the originator of the modern school of Jewish

58

interpretation], who applied it to the Jewish nation, the Messianic interpretation of this chapter was almost universally adopted by Jews, and his view, . . . was rejected as unsatisfactory by Maimonides, who is regarded by the Jews as of highest authority, by Alshech, and many others, one of whom [Rabbi Moshen Kohen Iben Crispin, of Cordova–fourteenth century] says that the interpretation adopted by Rashi 'distorts the passage from its natural meaning,' and that in truth 'it was given of God as a description of the Messiah, whereby, when any should claim to be the Messiah, to judge by the resemblance or non-resemblance to it whether he were the Messiah or no' . . . .[Crispin also said that those who apply the passage to Israel have 'forsaken the knowledge of our teachers, and inclined after . . . their own opinions.' (55:228)] And another [R. Elyyah de Vidas] says, 'The meaning of "he was wounded for our transgressions, . . . bruised for our iniquities" is, that since the Messiah bears our iniquities, which produce the effect of His being bruised, it follows that whoso will not admit that the Messiah thus suffers for our iniquities must endure and suffer for them himself.''' (55:225-229)

The father of modern Hebrew, Wilhelm Gesenius, has also written, "It was only the later Jews who abandoned this [Messianic] interpretation, no doubt in consequence of their controversies with the Christians." (52:II,295)

In brief, we agree with Gloag and Delitzsch: "All attempts to explain away this prophecy . . . have signally failed. It still stands as the most remarkable prediction in the Old Testament, receiving its accomplishment in the Messiah and in him alone." (52:II,116)

Even today, Dr. Pinchas Lapide, one of only four orthodox Jewish scholars in the world who is also a New Testament scholar has stated in a debate with Dr. Walter Kaiser on the John Ankerberg

59

Show: "I fully agree with Dr. Kaiser that Isaiah 53 lends itself in many startling similarities to the life, career and death of Jesus of Nazareth . . . ." (56:21) He even believes Jesus actually physically rose from the dead after being crucified because of the compelling historical facts. (70:7, 126-131, 137-150) Yet Dr. Lapide believes Jesus is the Messiah for the Gentiles and not for the Jews.

Let us ask you, If Jesus Christ is not God's suffering Servant found in Isaiah 53, then who is?

Who is the One that Eliazer Hakalir, a ninth century Jewish religious poet, wrote about when he paraphrased Isaiah 53 and put it into rhyme and metric poetry? This prayer was and has been a prayer from the traditional orthodox liturgy. Even today, (within certain elements of Judaism) it is recited on Yom Kippur, the Jewish Day of Atonement, in the prayer of Kether. But who else than Jesus of Nazareth could it be speaking about?

> "We are shrunk up in our misery even until now! Our Rock hath not come nigh to us; *Messiah* our Righteousness, hath turned from us; we are in terror, and there is none to justify us! *Our iniquities* and the yoke of *our transgressions He will bear*, for *He was wounded for our transgressions*; He will carry our sins upon His shoulder, that we may find forgiveness for our iniquities; and *by His stripes we are healed* . . . ." (105; 55:230, emphasis added)

Clues to Identify the Messiah

Whoever the Messiah is, He *must* fit the following descriptions:

Clue #1 – He, a male child (the Hebrew text specifically uses a 3rd person, singular, masculine pronoun – "he"), will be born of the seed of the woman.

Clue #2 – He will come from the race of the Jews, and specifically from the seed of Abraham, Isaac and Jacob.

Clue #3 – He will be a great prophet, with the authority to teach like Moses.

Clue #4 – He will be mocked, and people will cast lots for His garments while He suffers.

60

Clue #5 – He will be David's Lord.

Clue #6 – He will be the child born who is God, and will have an everlasting kingdom.

Clue #7 – He will be wounded and bruised, smitten and spit upon, mocked, killed with thieves, bear the sins of many, be rejected by His own people, pierced for our transgressions, be buried in a rich man's tomb, and come back to life after His death.

11. Jeremiah 23:5,6 – Who Is the Righteous Branch, the Wise King, Who Will Be Called "the Lord Our Righteousness"?

The Biblical Text

"Behold, the days come, says Jehovah, that I will raise to David a righteous Branch, and He will reign as King and act wisely, and shall do justice and righteousness in the earth. In his days Judah shall be saved, and Israel shall dwell safely. And this is his name (by) which he shall be called, Jehovah our righteousness." (Jeremiah 23:5-6)

The Context of the Passage

In this chapter God has pronounced judgment on the false leaders and prophets of Israel who were responsible for scattering and driving the people away from God (Jer. 23:1-2). God says that the evil practices of these false and lying prophets and the evil practices of the people themselves will result in their judgment (Jer. 23:9-27). We know from history and Scripture this divine judgment was the Babylonian captivity and exile. God now declares He will gather the remnant of His flock from all the countries and bring them back where they will be fruitful and increase in number. In doing so, He will place benevolent shepherds (leaders) over them who will protect and guide them so that they will no longer be afraid (Jer. 23:3-4).

It is at this point God states the amazing words found in verses 5 and 6 about the future. Someday He will raise up to David, a "righteous Branch," a "King," who will reign wisely and do what is just and right in the land. In his days, Judah will be saved and will live in safety. Then God specifically identifies this future Person by saying, *"This is the name by which he will be called, 'Jehovah our righteousness.'"*

The Explanation of the Text

Proof that this passage is speaking about the Messiah can be seen from the following:
(1) At least four other scriptural passages refer to a "Branch" who is acknowledged by many Jewish rabbis as being the Messiah

(Jer. 23:15; Isa. 4:2; Zech. 3:8; 6:12,13). Many have agreed that "this term [the Branch] is one of the proper names of the Messiah." (55:78, 90, 107, 116; 61:190)

(2) This person, the "Branch" is literally called "Jehovah our righteousness." This indicates that Messiah is somehow "God" (Jehovah).

(3) The Messiah is also stated to be "our righteousness." What this means we will see in a moment.

But first, who would dare claim to be "the Branch"? Who would dare utter he was "Jehovah"? Who would ever claim to be "Our Righteousness"?

There is only One Person in history who has claimed, *"Anyone who has seen me has seen the Father"* (Jn. 14:9, NIV). That One is Jesus Christ. He also declared, *"My Father, whom you claim is your God, is the One who glorifies me"* (Jn. 8:54, NIV). *"Before Abraham was born, I AM!"* (Jn. 8:58, NIV). *" 'We are not stoning you for any of these,' replied the Jews, 'but for blasphemy, because you, a mere man, claim to be God'"* (Jn. 10:33, NIV). The evidence clearly shows that men in Jesus' day understood He was claiming to be God.

What does this passage mean when it says this "Branch" out of David will be "Jehovah our righteousness"? We agree with Dr. Laestch who has compared other Messianic promises and concluded:

> "It is the righteousness which the Seed of David, who is the Woman's Seed of Gen. 3:15, procures for mankind by bruising Satan's head. As the Servant of the Lord, he bore the sins of man (Isa. 53:11), which the Lord laid on him (verse 6) who had done no wrong (verse 9) and who suffered all the penalties man had deserved (vv. 5-6). By his vicarious, substitutionary fulfillment of all the demands of the mandatory and punitive justice of God he became 'our righteousness,' establishing this righteousness as the norm to be followed in his kingdom. Since this righteousness was pro-

63

cured and established by him whom God calls 'Jehovah our righteousness,' it is a righteousness not only promised in the Old Testament, but as the righteousness procured by Jehovah it is as timeless as the Lord, retroactive (Heb. 9:15); . . . . It was counted as righteousness to believing Abraham (Gen. 15:6); it became the hope and trust and joy of all believers in the Old Testament (Heb. 11:1-40) . . . . It is that vicarious righteousness on account of which the Righteous Servant throughout the ages justifies many (Isa. 53:12), makes them righteous by declaring them righteous, children of God, heirs of salvation for the sake of the salvation he has procured. For this reason 'righteousness' is so frequently linked up with 'salvation.'" (61:191-192)

Let us ask, "Could all of this be true of anyone but Jesus Christ?" In Romans 3:21-26 we discover how Jehovah is our righteousness: *"But now a righteousness from God, apart from law, has been made known, to which the Law and the Prophets testify. This righteousness from God comes through faith in Jesus Christ to all who believe. There is no difference, for all have sinned and fall short of the glory of God, and are justified freely by his grace through the redemption that came by Christ Jesus. God presented him as a sacrifice of atonement, ... to demonstrate his justice at the present time, so as to be just and the one who justifies the man who has faith in Jesus"* (Rom. 3:21-26).

Was Jeremiah 23:5-6 Recognized by the Jews as Messianic?

The Targum of Isaiah reads, "I will raise up to David a righteous Messiah, a king who will reign wisely," proving the rabbis held this passage to be Messianic. (98:1160)

As Messianic experts have stated: "There is scarcely any contrary opinion among ancient and also modern Jews but that this is a Messianic prophecy." (55:78)

The great Rabbi David Kimchi (1160-1235 A.D.) was such a great scholar of the Hebrew Scriptures that the Jews had a saying

about him: "No Kimchi, no understanding of the Scriptures."
(55:19)

Concerning this verse, Rabbi Kimchi wrote, "By the righteous Branch is meant Messiah." (55:78) Those who wrote Targum Jonathan agreed with Kimchi. They introduced the Messiah by name in this passage. (55:78)

Hebrew scholar Alfred Edersheim quotes another rabbinic writing:

> "On Jer. xxiii, 5, 6, the Targum has it: 'And I will raise up for David the Messiah the Just.' This is one of the passages from which, according to Rabbinic views, one of the Names of the Messiah is derived, viz.: Jehovah our Righteousness. So in the Talmud (Babha Bathra 75b), in the Midrash on Ps. xxi. 1, Prov. xix. 21, and in that on Lamentations i. 16." (47:II,731)

In conclusion, this passage was clearly Messianic. It teaches the Messiah will be "Jehovah our righteousness" and in all of Israel's history, only Jesus Christ fits this description.

Clues to Identify the Messiah

Whoever the Messiah is, He *must* fit the following descriptions:

Clue #1 – He, a male child (the Hebrew text specifically uses a 3rd person, singular, masculine pronoun – "he"), will be born of the seed of the woman.

Clue #2 – He will come from the race of the Jews, and specifically from the seed of Abraham, Isaac and Jacob.

Clue #3 – He will be a great prophet, with the authority to teach like Moses.

Clue #4 – He will be mocked, and people will cast lots for His garments while He suffers.

Clue #5 – He will be David's Lord.

Clue #6 – He will be the child born who is God, and will have an everlasting kingdom.

Clue #7 – He will be wounded and bruised, smitten and spit upon, mocked, killed with thieves, bear the sins of many, be rejected by His own people, pierced for our transgressions, be buried in a rich man's tomb, and come back to life after His death.

Clue #8 – He will be Jehovah our Righteousness.

12. Daniel 9:24-27 – Who Is the "Anointed One" to Be "Cut Off" After 483 Years?

The Biblical Text

"Seventy 'weeks' are decreed for your people and your holy city to finish transgression, to put an end to sin, to atone for wickedness, to bring in everlasting righteousness, to seal up vision and prophecy and to anoint the Most Holy. Know and understand this: from the issuing of the decree to restore and rebuild Jerusalem until the Anointed One, the Ruler, comes, there will be seven 'weeks' and sixty-two 'weeks.' It will be rebuilt with streets and a trench, but in times of trouble. After the sixty-two 'weeks,' the Anointed One will be cut off and will have nothing. The people of the ruler who will come will destroy the city and the sanctuary."
(Daniel 9:24-26a)

The Context of the Passage

Daniel lived during the Babylonian captivity. He tells us he wrote this passage in the first year of the reign of King Darius, son of Xerxes (Dan. 9:1). From history we know that the reign of King Darius began in the year 538/537 B.C.

Daniel informed us that he was reading the Scriptures which had foretold both the Babylonian captivity and the return of the captive Israelites to their land. Thus, he says, *". . . I, Daniel, understood from the Scriptures, according to the word of the Lord given to Jeremiah the Prophet, that the desolation of Jerusalem would last seventy years"* (Dan. 9:2, NIV).

Jeremiah also stated, *"This whole land shall be a desolation and a horror and these nations shall serve the king of Babylon seventy years"* (Jer. 25:11, NAS). At the end of this time, the Lord said, *"When seventy years have been completed for Babylon, I will visit you and fulfill my good word to you, to bring you back to this place"* (Jer. 29:10, NAS).

Daniel had been involved in the first deportion to Babylon. It had happened in 605 B.C. when Nebuchadnezzar, son of

Nabopolassar, the king of Babylon, had invaded Palestine. Now, in 538 B.C. (67 years later), Daniel realized from Jeremiah that the 70-year captivity was nearing its completion.

He also realized the reason for Israel's captivity was their refusal to obey God (Jer. 29:17-19). The prophets had continually warned Israel about the consequences of seeking false gods and of ignoring God's commandments.

Specifically, Israel had ignored God's command to give the land a sabbatical rest (2 Chron. 36:20-21). God had stated that because of Israel's disobedience in this area, she would be removed from her land and scattered among the Gentiles until the land had enjoyed its sabbaths once more (Lev. 26:32-25).

According to Leviticus 25:2-5, a Sabbath year took place every seventh year. One year out of every seven was to be a year of rest for the land, a Sabbath to the Lord.

Because they had disobeyed, they were suffering one year of captivity for every Sabbath year they had neglected. Daniel realized the 70 years of punishment stood for each of the Sabbath years Israel had not kept over a 490-year period of time (490 years ÷ 70 disobedient Sabbaths = 70 years of captivity). Daniel concluded that before the exiles returned to their homeland, they needed to confess and repent of their sin of disobedience before God. He proceeded to confess the sins of the nation in prayer. At that point the angel Gabriel appeared and gave him the astonishing message about the Messiah in the future.

The Explanation of the Text

How do we know Gabriel's message to Daniel in this prophecy is about the Messiah? Because the Hebrew word that is used is "*Mashiach*" and must be translated "Messiah" or "the Anointed One." (22:833) As the great Princeton scholar Professor R. D. Wilson (who was fluent in 45 languages and dialects) states, "Daniel IX, 25,26 is one of the two [Hebrew] passages where the expected Savior of Israel is called *Messiah*." (107:II,138)

Yet some have objected to this view, claiming that rather than speaking of the "Messiah," the "Anointed One," Daniel is instead

68

referring to Cyrus, king of Persia. But this cannot apply to King Cyrus because, as we shall see, verses 25 and 26 declare that the "Messiah" will not arrive until some 400 years *after* Cyrus lived.

There have been others who have claimed "the Anointed One" is the Syrian ruler Antiochus Epiphanes. But this cannot be Antiochus since he died in 164 B.C. As we shall see, the prophecy talks about "the Messiah" coming to Jerusalem alive almost 200 years after that. Therefore, this One who is called "*Mashiach Nagid*" – Messiah the Prince – cannot refer to either Cyrus or to Antiochus Epiphanes. As Professor E. J. Young has said, "The non-Messianic interpretation is utterly inadequate." (106:193)

Who then is the Messiah who will come? Whoever the Messiah is, He will appear on the scene *after* the rebuilding of Jerusalem (Dan. 9:25-26) and be killed *before* Jerusalem and the temple are again destroyed.

In verses 25 and 26, the text states that once the decree is issued to restore and rebuild Jerusalem, the Messiah will come after 69 "weeks" (483 years – see below). Then, He will be "cut off and have nothing." The verb rendered "to cut off" has the meaning, "to destroy; to strike, to smite; to punish with death." (76:106) Leupold correctly states, "The verb used [here], (*karath*) . . . frequently refers to a form of violent death." (103:427)

Next, the angel tells Daniel that the Messiah will come after a period of time that he refers to as seven "weeks" plus 62 "weeks." "After the sixty-two weeks (i.e., after the 69th week – referring to that time which includes the seven previous weeks plus 62 weeks) the Messiah will be cut off."

But what is the meaning of the term "weeks"? For us today, the term "week" is restricted to mean a period of seven days. But the Hebrew word is not so restricted and instead stands for "units of seven." The Hebrew word that is used is *shabuim*, the plural form of the word *shabua*, translated as "sevens" in the NIV and as "weeks" in the NAS. As we shall see, the context must determine what "units of seven" is meant – whether it refers to units of "seven" days, weeks, years, etc.

69

In context Daniel 9:23-27 demands that the plural word *shabuim* must refer to units of seven *years*. Thus, Daniel would be speaking of 70 units, or periods of seven years, or a total of 490 years. Here are the reasons why the context of Daniel demands this conclusion:

1. Daniel tells us he has been thinking in terms of "years." He says in verse 2, *"I, Daniel, observed in the books the number of the 'years' which was revealed as the word of the Lord to Jeremiah . . ."* (Dan. 9:2).

2. Daniel had been considering the 70-year captivity. Each year of captivity represented one seven-year "period" or "unit" in which the Sabbath year had not been observed. Thus the context again is in reference to years, not to days.

3. In Daniel 10:2, 3, in the Hebrew text, Daniel carefully inserted the word "days" with *shabuim* to indicate the term weeks is referring to a period of seven *days*. But the fact that he deliberately excluded the word "days" with *shabuim* in Daniel 9 clearly indicates he did not intend to refer to days there. Rather, he was speaking about years. Dr. Alva McClain agrees. He has said, "[in Dan. 9:24-27] Daniel used the Hebrew *shabua* alone when referring to the well-known 'week' of years, a customary usage which every Jew would understand; but in chapter 10, when he speaks of the 'three weeks' of fasting, he definitely specifies them as 'weeks of *days*' in order to distinguish them from the 'weeks' of *years* in chapter 9." (44:20-21)

4. It would have been utterly impossible to restore and rebuild Jerusalem in seven literal weeks (Daniel 9:25 says the city will be rebuilt). Daniel must be referring to years. Again, the context demands seven units of seven "years" (or 49 years).

5. The term "*shabua*" has the meaning of "years" in the Mishna (17:117-118).

In light of these facts found in the context, Hoehner agrees, "the term *shabuim* in Daniel 9 most reasonably refers to a unit of seven years. To make it anything else does not make good sense." (17:118)

Now let's examine the meaning of this prophecy. Gabriel tells Daniel: *"You are to know and discern that from the issuing of a decree to restore and rebuild Jerusalem till Messiah the prince there will be seven weeks and sixty-two weeks; it will be built again, with plaza and moat, even in times of distress. Then after the sixty-two weeks, the Messiah will be cut off and have nothing . . . .''*

According to this, the Messiah will appear at the end of the 69 weeks (the seven weeks [49 years] plus 62 weeks [434 years] or a total of 483 years). After the 69 weeks (483 years) the destruction of the city and the temple will take place. (We know from history this took place in 70 A.D. under Titus and his Roman legions who destroyed Jerusalem.)

But from what year and what decree (the decree "to restore and rebuild Jerusalem") are we to begin to count the number of years until Messiah? There are four possibilities to consider.

First, it could not be Cyrus' edict issued in 539 B.C. (110:286; II Chron. 36:22) because Cyrus' command refers to the rebuilding of the temple and not to the city. Also, the inhabitants that occupied the city and rebuilt the temple did not erect natural defenses around the city to defend themselves. In other words, this was not a complete rebuilding of the city that was prophesied (vs. 25 says, "from the issuing of the decree to restore the rebuild **Jerusalem** . . . ").

Second, it could not be the decree given by Tattenai, governor of Judah, who made a search for Cyrus' decree and then issued a decree himself about 519/18 B.C. (Ezra 5:3-17). His decree simply confirmed Cyrus' and again only refers to the temple, *not* to the city.

The third decree was the decree of Artaxerxes to Ezra in 457 B.C. (17:126-129; 62:114; Ezra 7:12-26) But once again, this decree does not say one word about the rebuilding of the *city* of Jerusalem, only about the *temple* in Jerusalem.

The fourth decree was given by Artaxerxes to Nehemiah in 444 B.C. (17:126-128; Neh. 2:1-8) In all probability, this is the decree to rebuild Jerusalem that Gabriel described to Daniel and which began the seventy weeks of time. Most importantly, in Artaxerxes' decree to Nehemiah, there is a direct reference to the restoration of the city and of the city gates and walls (Gabriel said in vs. 25 Jerusalem *"will be rebuilt with streets **and a trench**"* [actually a moat, a defensive structure, going around the outside of the city]).

In addition, Artaxerxes wrote a letter to Asaph specifically asking for materials which would be used to build the walls of Jerusalem (Neh. 2:8). In the book of Nehemiah and Ezra we are told that the restoration of the walls was done in the most distressing circumstances (Eze. 4:7-23) – exactly as predicted by Daniel (Dan. 9:25). No later decrees were given by the Persian kings pertaining to the rebuilding of Jerusalem.

Finally, we are ready to determine how long it was from the decree of Artaxerxes (444 B.C.) until after the 69th week (483 years later) when Gabriel announced the Messiah would be killed in Jerusalem. It turns out to be 33 A.D., the very time in which Jesus Christ lived and was crucified in Jerusalem! (For those who wish a more detailed analysis as to how we arrived at these dates, see Appendix Two.)

The important point in this prophetic passage is this: clearly, the Messiah had to come by the end of the 69th week, 483 years later. Remember, the time between the decree authorizing Jerusalem to be rebuilt (verse 25 – 444 B.C.) and the coming of the Messiah, was to be 69 "sevens" (7 + 62 = 69 × 7) or 483 years. That is the exact time that Jesus Christ was alive and ministering.

Again, Jesus Christ is the *only possible* candidate to be the Jewish Messiah. No other person of any period, or for that matter in human history, (1) claimed to be the Messiah, (2) fulfilled such detailed Messianic prophecies made hundreds of years in advance and (3) rose from the dead to prove the truth of His claims and Person.

Was Daniel 9:24-27 Recognized by the Jews as Messianic?

Since this text explicitly speaks of the Messiah it would be difficult for Jewish rabbis to deny it. Still, because this prophecy predicted the Messiah was to be "cut off" (die), some denied that it referred to the Messiah. (52:II,223)

But, on the other hand, many rabbis boldly stated this passage predicted the time of the Messiah's appearing so exactly that if

Christ was not the Messiah, then Israel had no Messiah. Further, if Messiah was to come, it had to be at the exact same time period as that in which Christ lived.

The Talmud advises, "In Daniel is delivered to us the end ['the time of His appearance and death' – Rabbi Jarchi] of the Messiah." (52:II,226)

The Talmud records that at about the time of Titus (70 A.D.) it was believed that the Messiah had already come. But His appearance was concealed from the Jews until they were rendered more worthy of His appearance. (52:II,226)

Rabbi Nehumias, who lived some *50 years before* Christ, is cited by Grotius as saying that the time fixed by Daniel for the Messiah could not go beyond fifty years. (52:II,226)

Clues to Identify the Messiah

Whoever the Messiah is, He *must* fit the following descriptions:

Clue #1 – He, a male child (the Hebrew text specifically uses a 3rd person, singular, masculine pronoun – "he"), will be born of the seed of the woman.

Clue #2 – He will come from the race of the Jews, and specifically from the seed of Abraham, Isaac and Jacob.

Clue #3 – He will be a great prophet, with the authority to teach like Moses.

Clue #4 – He will be mocked, and people will cast lots for His garments while He suffers.

Clue #5 – He will be David's Lord.

Clue #6 – He will be the child born who is God, and will have an everlasting kingdom.

Clue #7 – He will be wounded and bruised, smitten and spit upon, mocked, killed with thieves, bear the sins of many, be rejected by His own people, pierced for our transgressions, be buried in a rich man's tomb, and come back to life after His death.

Clue #8 – He will be Jehovah our Righteousness.

Clue #9 – He will be the Messiah who comes to Jerusalem 483 years after the decree to rebuild Jerusalem is given. At that time He will be killed.

13. Micah 5:2 – Who Is the One Who Is Eternal, Who Will Be the Ruler over Israel, Who Is Born in Bethlehem Ephrathah?

The Biblical Text

"But you Bethlehem Ephrathah, though you are least among the thousands of Judah, out of you He shall come forth to Me to be ruler in Israel, His goings forth have been from old, from the days of eternity." (Micah 5:2)

The Context of the Passage

Micah Chapter 5 begins with a statement of doom concerning a siege laid against Israel and its ruler. It is immediately followed by a statement of hope, the foretelling of a future King who will bring lasting security to Israel and whose influence will extend to all the earth. (62:427)

Note that the prophecy is specific. It identifies Bethlehem as "Ephrathah" (the older name for Bethlehem – Gen. 35:16,19; 48:7; Ruth 1:2; 4:11) – which distinguishes this Bethlehem from other towns named Bethlehem such as the one in Zebulun (Josh. 19:15).

Use of the term "Ephrathah" also identifies Bethlehem as the town in which David was born (1 Sam. 17:12) further establishing the Messianic connection between the Messiah and King David's throne. (62:427)

The Explanation of the Text

Grammatically, the term "from ancient times" must apply to the ruler from the days of eternity. (62:427) This ruler's activities are said to stem from the ancient past, yet his coming is still future.

The term "old" literally means from "ancient time, aforetime." The word "old" (*qedem*) is used of God Himself on occasion in the Old Testament (Deut. 33:27; Hab. 1:12). The words "from the days of eternity" (*mee mai-oulom*) literally mean from "ancient time or eternity." Both "old" and "ancient times" can

74

thus refer to eternity. The Hebrew word for "ancient times" is used in Micah 4:7 where it says, *"And Jehovah shall reign over them . . . forever [eternally]."*

The fact that such terms were used of a future ruler indicates that Micah expected a supernatural figure. This harmonizes with Isaiah's expectation of the Messiah in Isaiah 9:6 where the future Messianic King is called "eternal" and "God" (El), a word Isaiah uses only of God. (62:427) Hailey comments that the words "from old, from ancient times" "indicate more than that he descends from an ancient lineage; it relates Him to God, the Eternal One. His rule reaches back into eternity." (63:209)

The meaning of this verse revolves around two key points:
(1.) Like his ancestor King David, this future ruler of Israel will be born in insignificant Bethlehem.
(2.) His goings forth, His activities, extend back into eternity.

According to the scholar Hengstenberg, the Prophet Micah describes, "first, the existence of the Messiah before his birth in time, in Bethlehem, is pointed out in general; and *then*, in contrast with all time, it is vindicated to eternity. This could not fail to afford a great consolation to Israel. He who hereafter, in a visible manifestation, was to deliver them from their misery, was already in existence, – during it, before it, and through all eternity." (22:358-359)

Jesus Christ was born in Bethlehem 700 years later.

Was Micah 5:2 Recognized by the Jews as Messianic?

This book has long been acknowledged as Messianic. Gloag remarks that:

> All the ancient Jewish interpreters adhere to the Messianic meaning . . . . So also the testimony of the Targums is in favor of the Messianic interpretation of the prophecy. Thus the Targum of Jonathan says: 'And thou, Bethlehem of Ephrathtah, little art thou to be reckoned among the thousands of the house of Judah; out of thee shall proceed in my presence the Messiah to

75

exercise sovereignty over Israel; whose name has been called from eternity, from the days of the everlasting.' 'Thou art little,' observes Rabbi Jarchi, 'But out of thee shall come forth to me King Messiah.' " (52:II,118-119)

Edersheim states that among the rabbis, "The well-known passage, Micah 5:2, is admittedly Messianic. So [also] in the Targum, . . . and by later Rabbis." (47:735)

That the Jews recognized this as a Messianic prophecy is also evident from the fact that the priests and scribes of Herod's day knew that the Messiah would be born in Bethlehem on the basis of this prophecy (Mt. 2:5, 6). Thus, the common Jewish belief at the time of Christ was that they "unanimously regarded this passage as containing a prophecy of the birth of the Messiah in Bethlehem." (64:481) This is proven by Matthew 2:5, 6 and John 7:42.

Clues to Identify the Messiah

Whoever the Messiah is, He *must* fit the following descriptions:

Clue #1 – He, a male child (the Hebrew text specifically uses a 3rd person, singular, masculine pronoun – "he"), will be born of the seed of the woman.

Clue #2 – He will come from the race of the Jews, and specifically from the seed of Abraham, Isaac and Jacob.

Clue #3 – He will be a great prophet, with the authority to teach like Moses.

Clue #4 – He will be mocked, and people will cast lots for His garments while He suffers.

Clue #5 – He will be David's Lord.

Clue #6 – He will be the child born who is God, and will have an everlasting kingdom.

Clue #7 – He will be wounded and bruised, smitten and spit upon, mocked, killed with thieves, bear the sins of many, be rejected by His own people, pierced for our transgressions, be buried in a rich man's tomb, and come back to life after His death.

Clue #8 – He will be Jehovah our Righteousness.

Clue #9 – He will be the Messiah who comes to Jerusalem 483 years after the decree to rebuild Jerusalem is given. At that time He will be killed.

Clue #10 – He will be born in Bethlehem but has existed eternally.

14. Zechariah 9:9 – Who Is the King of Jerusalem, "Righteous and Having Salvation" Who Comes "Gentle and Riding on a Donkey"?

The Biblical Text

"Rejoice greatly, O daughter of Zion! Shout, O daughter of Jerusalem! Behold! your King comes to you! He is righteous and having salvation, gentle and riding on a donkey, on a colt, the foal of a donkey." (Zechariah 9:9)

The Context of the Passage

This verse occurs in the context of God's judgment on Israel's enemies and the promise of Israel's coming King.

The Explanation of the Text

"Perhaps in no other single book in the Old Testament scriptures is Messiah's Divinity so clearly taught as in Zechariah." (55:77) The prophet in Chapter 2:9, 10 has already stated that God Himself would live among the Jewish people – " *'Shout and be glad, O daughter of Zion. For I am coming, and I will live among you,'* declares the Lord."

Now, according to Zechariah 9:9, there will be a Messianic King, who is "righteous and having salvation," who will enter Jerusalem. It says He will be "gentle and riding on a donkey." Who else but Jesus Christ ever claimed He was righteous and had salvation (Jn. 3:16, 18; 5:24, 34, 39; 8:29, 46)? Who else claimed that He was the personal fulfillment of this prophecy and entered the city of Jerusalem, gentle and riding on a donkey (Jn. 12:13-16; Mt. 21:1-11)?

Was Zechariah 9:9 Recognized by the Jews as Messianic?

The Jews accepted this Scripture as a Messianic prophecy. For example, Delitzsch and Gloag observe, "This prophecy cannot possibly refer to Zerubbabel, or to any Jewish monarch or ruler after the time of Zechariah; but can only have a reference to the Anointed King, or the Messiah. This the Jews themselves are constrained to admit. 'It is impossible,' observes rabbi Jarchi, 'to expound this text of any other than the Messiah.'" (52:II,119)

It is a fact that Jesus entered Jerusalem triumphantly, riding on the colt of a donkey (Mt. 21:6-11).

Clues to Identify the Messiah

Whoever the Messiah is, He **must** fit the following descriptions:

Clue #1 – He, a male child (the Hebrew text specifically uses a 3rd person, singular, masculine pronoun – "he"), will be born of the seed of the woman.

Clue #2 – He will come from the race of the Jews, and specifically from the seed of Abraham, Isaac and Jacob.

Clue #3 – He will be a great prophet, with the authority to teach like Moses.

Clue #4 – He will be mocked, and people will cast lots for His garments while He suffers.

Clue #5 – He will be David's Lord.

Clue #6 – He will be the child born who is God, and will have an everlasting kingdom.

Clue #7 – He will be wounded and bruised, smitten and spit upon, mocked, killed with thieves, bear the sins of many, be rejected by His own people, pierced for our transgressions, be buried in a rich man's tomb, and come back to life after His death.

Clue #8 – He will be Jehovah our Righteousness.

Clue #9 – He will be the Messiah who comes to Jerusalem 483 years after the decree to rebuild Jerusalem is given. At that time He will be killed.

Clue #10 – He will be born in Bethlehem but has existed eternally.

Clue #11 – He will be the King, who has salvation and comes riding on a donkey.

15. Zechariah 12:10 – Who Is Jehovah, "the One They Have Pierced" for Whom Jerusalem and All the Nation of Israel Will Weep and Mourn?

The Biblical Text

*"And I will pour on the house of David, and on the inhabitants of Jerusalem, the spirit of grace and of prayers. And they shall look on **Me** whom they have pierced, and they shall mourn for **Him**, as one mourns for an only son, and they shall be bitter over Him, as one that is in bitterness over the firstborn."* (Zech. 12:10, emphasis added)

The Context of the Passage

This text says God will pour out His Spirit on Israel and bring them to a painful understanding sometime in the future. What will they understand? This is one of the most amazing statements given by God in Scripture. He says, *"[They] will look on me, the one they have pierced, and mourn for Him as one mourns for an only child . . ."* The question is, who is this One that Israel will look on and begin to mourn?

The Explanation of the Text

Zechariah is relating the words of Jehovah God, who says, *"They will look on Me whom they have pierced."* Jehovah Himself claims to be the One Israel has pierced. When did Israel pierce Jehovah?

In the middle of the statement, *"They will look on Me, the one they have pierced, and they shall mourn for Him,"* the pronouns are significantly changed. They refer to different persons. What was at first a reference to Jehovah, now becomes a reference to an unidentified "him" that the entire nation of Israel will mourn for. Delitzsch and Gloag explain:

"The great difficulty in this passage is occasioned by the change in the pronouns; it is said, 'They shall look upon me whom they have pierced, and they shall mourn for Him', as if two persons were spoken of – the one, the Lord, whom the inhabitants of Jerusalem have pierced; and the other, some unkown person, whose death the inhabitants of Jerusalem lament." (52:II,120)

They further comment:

"Some endeavor to escape the Messianic application of the prediction by supposing that the word 'pierced' is to be taken in a metaphorical sense, ...But it is doubtful if the word can be taken in this . . .sense; it denotes 'to thrust through,' 'to pierce as with a spear.' Besides, the mourning here is expressed as the mourning for the dead: One 'mourning for his only son, and in bitterness for his first born,' " (52:II,121)

Because of this passage, certain questions must be answered. They are: (1) If the Hebrew word for "to pierce," is "to thrust through, to slay by death," (108:388) when did Israel slay Jehovah? And how could the Creator of the heaven and the earth be slain by men? And when was this done?

Zechariah says Israel will someday realize they have killed Him – Jehovah, and will begin to mourn over Him as a family would mourn over the death of their only son.

This prophecy only fits Jesus Christ. Why? Jesus Christ is the only One who ever claimed to be God, claimed to be the Messiah, and was crucified by the inhabitants of Jerusalem.

Jews in the New Testament recognized only Jesus fit the words of this verse. The Apostle John wrote, *"In the beginning was the Word, and the Word was with God and the Word was God . . . . And the Word became flesh and dwelt among us, and we beheld his glory, glory as of the only begotten from the Father, full of grace and truth"* (Jn. 1:1, 14). Jesus Christ was the very incarnation of God.

81

The Apostle Paul believed Jesus was God and that He volunteered to die for our sins. Paul taught, *"Who [Jesus], being in very nature God, . . . made Himself nothing, taking the very nature of a servant, . . . and being found in appearance as a man, he humbled Himself and became obedient to death – even death on a cross!"* (Phil. 2:6-8).

The Apostle Peter must have been thinking of Zechariah's prophecy when on Pentecost he said, *"Therefore let all Israel be assured of this: God has made this Jesus, whom you crucified, both Lord and Christ [Messiah]"* (Acts 2:46).

Related to this, some wrongly teach that only the Jewish people are responsible for crucifying the Messiah. Apparently, they have **not** read where the New Testament Scriptures record, *"Indeed, Herod and Pontius Pilate met together **with the Gentiles and the people of Israel** in this city to conspire against your holy servant Jesus, whom you anointed"* (Acts 4:27). Both Jew and Gentile, all of us are equally guilty of crucifying Christ. Also, Jesus, being God, volunteered to die on the cross to pay the penalty for our sins. His death was for each one of us. In a real sense, all of our sins put Him there.

But let us ask, Who else but Jesus Christ could the Prophet Zechariah be speaking about? Who else could possibly be Jehovah, and also claim to be thrust through and killed by the inhabitants of Jerusalem? Remember, the word "pierce" is a word which means "to pierce as with a spear." (52:II,121) This is exactly what happened to Jesus on the cross. A spear was thrust through His side (Jn. 19:32, 35).

Finally, it says that the entire nation will mourn and grieve bitterly over the death of this One who has been pierced, "as one mourns for an only child." Would the Jewish people mourn for this One as for the death of their only son, if He wasn't actually one of their Jewish sons – as Jesus Christ was?

What if the Jewish people someday come to recognize, after all these centuries of rejecting Him, that Jesus really was their Messiah? What if they come to understand who He really is? What if they someday look upon Him as God, "the One whom they have pierced"? Wouldn't Zechariah's prophecy be fulfilled? Wouldn't there be great weeping in Jerusalem?

Remember, God pours out His Spirit on His people so people will come to know His true Messiah, who loved them so much He gave His life (was pierced through) for them. As Isaiah said, *"the Lord laid on Him the iniquities of us all"* (Is. 53:6).

Was Zechariah 12:10 Recognized by the Jews as Messianic?

That this prophecy refers to the Messiah was admitted by the rabbis. (109:199) For example, this prophecy "is applied to the Messiah the Son of Joseph in the Talmud (Sukk.52a) and so is verse 12, . . ." (47:737)

Thus, some Jewish interpreters, trying to avoid the clear implication of the words, have attempted to apply this passage to the "other" Messiah who would suffer, Messiah Ben Jospeh.

> ". . . the later interpreters explaining it of Messiah Ben Joseph, or the suffering Messiah, whom they invented to meet the passages of Scripture that speak so clearly of this characteristic of the promised Redeemer. But as they believed that this Messiah son of Joseph was a mere man, the difficulty met them that Jehovah declared 'they shall look on ME whom they have pierced;' so that if it refers to the Messiah he cannot be a mere man, but must be divine." (109:199-200)

In spite of this, when Jehovah says, *"they will look on Me, the one they have pierced,"* this prophecy uniquely fits only Jesus Christ.

Clues to Identify the Messiah

Whoever the Messiah is, He *must* fit the following descriptions:

Clue #1 – He, a male child (the Hebrew text specifically uses a 3rd person, singular, masculine pronoun – "he"), will be born of the seed of the woman.

Clue #2 – He will come from the race of the Jews, and specifically from the seed of Abraham, Isaac and Jacob.

83

Clue #3 – He will be a great prophet, with the authority to teach like Moses.

Clue #4 – He will be mocked, and people will cast lots for His garments while He suffers.

Clue #5 – He will be David's Lord.

Clue #6 – He will be the child born who is God, and will have an everlasting kingdom.

Clue #7 – He will be wounded and bruised, smitten and spit upon, mocked, killed with thieves, bear the sins of many, be rejected by His own people, pierced for our transgressions, be buried in a rich man's tomb, and come back to life after His death.

Clue #8 – He will be Jehovah our Righteousness.

Clue #9 – He will be the Messiah who comes to Jerusalem 483 years after the decree to rebuild Jerusalem is given. At that time He will be killed.

Clue #10 – He will be born in Bethlehem but has existed eternally.

Clue #11 – He will be the King, who has salvation and comes riding on a donkey.

Clue #12 – He will be Jehovah, the One pierced by the inhabitants of Jerusalem.

16. Malachi 3:1 – When Did God Suddenly Come to His Temple? Who Was the Messenger He Sent before Him to Prepare the Way?

The Biblical Text

" 'Behold, I am sending My messenger, and he shall prepare the way before Me. And the Lord, whom you seek, shall suddenly come to His temple, even the Angel of the Covenant, in whom you delight. Behold, He comes,' says Jehovah of hosts.'' (Malachi 3:1)

The Context of the Passage

In Malachi 2:17, the people of Israel, immersed in their own miseries, complained and asked, *"Where is the God of justice?"* Malachi's response was simple: *"The Lord whom you seek will suddenly come to his temple"* (3:1).

However, before He would come, God would send a "forerunner" to prepare the way ahead of Him. The text does not say *a* messenger, but *His* messenger.

The people of Israel were already familiar with this "forerunner" from Isaiah's prophecy in Isaiah 40:3 where the Hebrew words, "To prepare the way," are identical with those used here in Malachi 3:1.

It was necessary that mankind be morally prepared for the coming of the Lord. The messenger of the Covenant who would come to His temple would be none other than the Lord God Himself. The word "Lord" here (*ha adon*) always refers to God (cf. Isaiah 1:24; 3:1; 10:16, 33).

The Explanation of the Text

Malachi's prophecy is quoted in the New Testament in Matthew 11:10, Mark 1:2 and Luke 7:27 where the messenger preparing the way before God is John the Baptist. Jesus Christ Himself said about John the Baptist in Matthew 11:10, *"This is the one about whom it is written: 'I will send my messenger ahead of you, who will prepare your way before you.'"*

But who is "the Lord . . . the Angel of the Covenant" that suddenly comes to His temple? Who else could this be referring to but Jesus Christ? Concerning the term "the Angel of the Covenant" Lange writes:

> "From a very early period we find mention of an extraordinary Messenger, or Angel, who is sometimes called the 'Angel of God,' at others, the 'Angel of Jehovah.' He is represented as the Mediator between the invisible God and men in all God's communications and dealings with men. To this Angel divine names, attributes, purposes, and acts are ascribed. He occasionally assumed a human form, as in his interviews with Hagar, Abraham, Jacob, Joshua, Gideon, Manoah, and his wife. He went before the camp of Israel on the night of the exodus. In Exodus 23:20, Jehovah said, 'Behold, I send an angel before thee to bring thee into the place, which I have prepared. My name is in him.' In Isaiah 63:9 he is called 'the angel of his Presence, or face,' where there is a reference to Exodus 33:14, 15, where Jehovah said to Moses, 'My Presence (or Hebrew, My face) shall go with thee,' and Moses said, 'if thy face go not with us, carry us not up hence.' He is called the 'face of God,' because though no man can see his face and live, yet the Angel of his face is the brightness of his glory, and the express image of his person. In him Jehovah's presence is manifested, and his glory reflected, for the glory of God shines in the face of Jesus Christ. There is thus a gradual development in the Old Testament of the doctrine of the incarnation, of the distinction of persons in the Godhead, not brought to light fully, lest it should interfere with the doctrine of the unity of God." (115:19)

The questions which this text raise are: When did the Lord suddenly come to His temple? Who is the Angel of the Covenant? Who else could it have been but Jesus Christ?

Was Malachi 3:1 Recognized by the Jews as Messianic?

"The Messianic character of this verse is generally allowed by Jewish and Christian writers, however they may attempt to explain it." (52:II,122) Edersheim observes, "this passage is applied to Elijah as forerunner of the Messiah in Pirqe de R. Eliz. C.29." (47:736)

Clues to Identify the Messiah

Whoever the Messiah is, He *must* fit the following descriptions:

Clue #1 – He, a male child (the Hebrew text specifically uses a 3rd person, singular, masculine pronoun – "he"), will be born of the seed of the woman.

Clue #2 – He will come from the race of the Jews, and specifically from the seed of Abraham, Isaac and Jacob.

Clue #3 – He will be a great prophet, with the authority to teach like Moses.

Clue #4 – He will be mocked, and people will cast lots for His garments while He suffers.

Clue #5 – He will be David's Lord.

Clue #6 – He will be the child born who is God, and will have an everlasting kingdom.

Clue #7 – He will be wounded and bruised, smitten and spit upon, mocked, killed with thieves, bear the sins of many, be rejected by His own people, pierced for our transgressions, be buried in a rich man's tomb, and come back to life after His death.

Clue #8 – He will be Jehovah our Righteousness.

Clue #9 – He will be the Messiah who comes to Jerusalem 483 years after the decree to rebuild Jerusalem is given. At that time He will be killed.

Clue #10 – He will be born in Bethlehem but has existed eternally.

Clue #11 – He will be the King, who has salvation and comes riding on a donkey.

Clue #12 – He will be Jehovah, the One pierced by the inhabitants of Jerusalem.

Clue #13 – The Lord Himself will actually come to the temple in Jerusalem, but be preceded by a messenger.

We may summarize what we have learned so far. So far, we have seen that a male seed of the woman will defeat Satan but be wounded in the process. This seed will be a descendant of Abraham, then Isaac, then Jacob. In this coming One, all of the world will be blessed. He will be unique in all of Israel's history, because He will be a "prophet like Moses." But He will be mocked, insulted and crucified by men. Surprisingly, His bones will not be broken, but His garments will be gambled for. Although He will be a descendant of king David, He will also be David's "Lord" and be second only to God Himself. He will be a child given to Israel who will also be God, who will have an everlasting kingdom, and who will live in Galilee. In addition, this coming One will be perfectly innocent and yet He will die for the world's sins. But He will come back to life from the dead in resurrection. He is given a specific name, "Jehovah our Righteousness." He will arrive exactly 483 years after the 444 B.C. decree of Artaxerxes to Nehemiah to rebuild Jerusalem. He will be the ruler of Israel who is "the eternal One Himself," and yet He will be *born* in Bethlehem! He will be the very King of Israel who will bring salvation, but surprisingly – He will come riding on a donkey. In addition, He will be Jehovah Himself who will be "pierced," and all Israel will mourn for Him.

Finally, we see that this coming One, the Messiah of Israel, will suddenly come to His temple but that a special messenger will be sent before Him to prepare His way.

If we look at all these prophecies we see that Jesus Christ has fulfilled all of them:

Genesis 3:15 – Jesus defeated Satan but was wounded during the crucifixion.

Genesis 12, 17, 22 – He was the literal descendant of Abraham, Isaac and Jacob in whom all the world was blessed.

Deuteronomy 18 – He was the "prophet like Moses."

Psalm 22 – He was mocked, insulted and crucified. His garments were gambled for and His bones were not broken.

Psalm 1:10 – He was David's "Lord."

Isaiah 9 – He was God Himself and He lived in Galilee.

Isaiah 53 – He was perfectly innocent and without sin, yet He atoned for the sin of the world. He was resurrected from the dead.

Jeremiah 23 – Because He was God and "justified many," His proper name is "Jehovah our Righteousness."

Daniel 9 – He arrived at the specific time given by the prophecy, 483 years after Artaxerxes' decree to rebuild Jerusalem.

Micah 5 – He was eternal and He was born in Bethlehem.

Zechariah 9 – He was the King of Israel who brought salvation and

He entered Jerusalem riding on a donkey.

Zechariah 12 – He was Jehovah, He was pierced.

Malachi 3 – John the Baptist prepared the way for Him as He suddenly came to His temple.

We have examined just a few of the prophecies concerning the Messiah found in the Hebrew Scriptures. Had we space, there are dozens of others which we could have discussed that are just as specific as these.

(1) He will be born of a virgin (Isa. 7:14; see Mt. 1:23).

(2) He would live in Nazareth of Galilee (Isa. 9:1-2; see Mt. 2:23; 4:15).

(3) He would occasion the massacre of Bethlehem's children (Jer. 31:15; see Mt. 2:18).

(4) His mission would include the Gentiles (Isa. 42:1-3, 6; see Mt. 12:18-21).

(5) His ministry would include physical relief (Isa. 61:1-2; see Lk. 4:16-21).

(6) He would be the Shepherd struck with the sword, resulting in the sheep being scattered (Zech. 13:7; see Mt. 26:31, 56; Mk. 14:27, 49-50).

(7) He would be betrayed by a friend for 30 pieces of silver (Zech. 11:12-13; see Mt. 27:9-10).

(8) He would be given vinegar and gall to drink (Ps. 69:21; see Mt. 27:34).

(9) He would be presented with all dominion over all peoples, nations and men of every language (Dan. 7:13-14; see Rev. 11:15).

(10) He would be hated without a cause (Ps. 69:4; Isa. 49:7; Jn. 7:48; Jn. 15:25).

(11) He would be rejected by the rulers (Ps. 118:22; Mt. 21:42; Jn. 7:48).

But the point should be obvious. Who is the only Person who has fulfilled all of these prophecies and more? Only Jesus Christ. There is no way to avoid this fact.

Scholars Delitzsch and Gloag have rightly stated:

"So far as we can determine, these prophecies refer to the Messiah only, and cannot be predicated of another. The ancient Jews admit the Messianic character of most of them; although the modern Jews, in consequence of their controversy with the Christians, have attempted to explain them away by applications which must appear to every candid reader to be unnatural . . . these and other predictions have received their accomplishment in Jesus of Nazareth, . . . the combination of prophecies is sufficient to prove that Jesus is the Messiah; . . ." (52:123-124)

17. The Uniqueness of the Messianic Prophecies

The uniqueness of the Messianic prophecies is seen in the following facts:

(1) Despite the vast time period and the large number of authors who have prophesied about the Messiah, the prophecies form a united and progressive revelation that is not contradictory.

(2) The Messianic prophecies are minute and specific in detail.

(3) Their content is unique in all of religious literature.

(4) Their fulfillment has been exact, but only in the Person of Jesus, not in any other prophet or events of Israel's history.

(5) The events predicted were not expected and could never have been foreseen by men. This is evident from their number, combination and complexity.

(6) The prophecies were written hundreds of years before the events occurred.

It is only logical to conclude that if these Messianic prophecies were written hundreds of years before they occurred, and if they could never have been foreseen and depended upon factors outside human control for their fulfillment, and if *all* of these prophecies perfectly fit the Person and life of Jesus Christ, then Jesus had to be the Messiah.

This conclusion can be avoided only by denying that the prophecies exist, or denying that Jesus fulfilled them. The prophecies do exist, and even skeptics (whether or not they accept Him as Messiah) admit that they remarkably fit the life of Jesus.

After understanding the uniqueness of these prophecies and seeing their clear connection to Jesus Christ, you may wonder how anyone would still not be persuaded that Jesus is God's Messiah.

Well, some still do deny this evidence and we will now look at their objections and briefly answer them.

18. Why the Jews Rejected Their Messiah

As Alfred Edersheim observes in his monumental work, *The Life and Times of Jesus the Messiah*, "The general conception which the rabbis *had formed* of the Messiah, differed totally from what was presented by the prophet of Nazareth [Jesus]." (47:I,160; cf. II,741) (Emphasis added.)

The rabbis' modern picture of the Messiah contradicts much of their own scriptural commentaries down through history (such as the Midrashic and Talmudic commentaries.) What is significant is that their own scriptural commentary paints a picture of the Messiah which fits none other than Jesus Christ.

How did they arrive at their modern interpretation which differs with their historial commentaries? Part of the problem was that they saw the Messiah everywhere in the Old Testament. Edersheim comments,

> "And perhaps the most valuable element in rabbinic commentation on Messianic times is that in which, as so frequently, it is explained, that all the miracles and deliverances of Israel's past would be reenacted – only in a much wider manner, in the days of the Messiah. *Thus the whole past was symbolic, and typical of the future* – the Old Testament the glass, through which the universal blessings of the latter days were seen. It is in this sense that we would understand the two sayings of the Talmud: 'All the prophets prophesied only of the days of the Messiah,' and 'the world was created only for the Messiah.'" (47:I,162,163)

Because the rabbis saw the Messiah everywhere in the Old Testament, they were able to choose from a variety of materials and form a selected picture of the Messiah that would cater to their needs. As Gloag remarks,

> "According to their interpretation of the Messianic prophecies, the Messiah was to be an earthly Prince who would sit upon the throne of David, rescue the Jews from the bondage and tyranny of

Rome, restore the kingdom to Israel, and subdue their enemies. Entertaining such expectations, filled with such hopes, giving such an interpretation to the Messianic prophecies, it is no matter of surprise that they could not see their fulfillment in One whose life and character and fate were so opposite to those of their expected Messiah." (52:324)

There can be no doubt that the amount of Messianic material in the Hebrew Scriptures that the rabbis have to evaluate is substantial. Edersheim has painstakingly (47:II, 710ff) analyzed some 456 Old Testament passages which the ancient Jews deemed Messianic. Of these, 75 were from the Pentateuch, 243 from the prophets and 138 from the Hagiographa or the Writings. In addition, he cites over 558 references supporting their Messianic application. (47:I,163) Even with all of this, he tells us this is an incomplete list. (47:II,710)

After analyzing the rabbinic commentaries on the Messianic passages noted above, Edersheim concluded:

"Accordingly, a careful perusal of their [456] scripture quotations shows, that the main postulates of the New Testament concerning the Messiah are fully *supported by rabbinic statements*. Thus, such doctrines as the *pre-mundane existence* of the Messiah; his *elevation* above Moses, and even above the Angels; his *representative* character; his cruel *suffering* and *derision*; his *violent death*, and that *for his people*; his *work* on behalf of the living and of the dead; his *redemption* and restoration of Israel; the *opposition* of the gentiles; their partial *judgment* and *conversion*; the *prevalence* of his *Law*; the *universal blessings* of the latter days; and his *kingdom* – can be clearly deduced from unquestioned passages in ancient rabbinic writings . . . . There is, indeed, in rabbinic writings frequent reference to the sufferings, and even the death of the Messiah, and these are brought into connection with our sins – as how

93

could it be otherwise in view of Isaiah LIII. and other passages – . . . ." (47:I,164-165) (First emphasis ours.)

Edersheim's underlining was to show that it was Jesus Christ who met the rabbinic expectations in these areas.

But if the portrait of Jesus was there in the rabbinical writings, what other reasons distorted the rabbis' picture of the Messiah? Besides the reasons already referred to, almost all of the Jewish commentaries were not open to accepting the idea of the removal of sin through the vicarious atonement and suffering of the Messiah.

That the idea of a suffering Messiah was not readily accepted is understandable. It detracted from their idea of a kingly Messiah. In addition, the Jews as a whole did not place a great emphasis on the concept of original sin and the utter sinfulness of human nature, even though it is in their Scriptures. (47:I, 165) Thus, it was difficult for them to conceive of the Messiah as being an atoning sin-bearer. (47:I, 167)

Another major reason the rabbis missed the true picture of the Messiah was because of the unthinkable idea that the Messiah would actually be both God and man in one person. That is why in the Gospels we see the Jews attempting to stone Jesus to death for claiming to be Messiah and God (e.g., Jn. 10:30-33).

Yet ironically, the Jews' own concept of the Messiah revealed in their Scriptures was far above human and even angelic status. (For example, the Messiah was acknowledged in their commentaries as eternal because of Isaiah 9:6 and Micah 5:2 – 47:I,171-172.) Because of this high view of the Messiah in their rabbinic commentaries, once the reality of Jesus' Messiahship was seen, His dual nature (both God and man) was readily accepted by first century Jews who became Christians. (47:I, 165-172)

In conclusion, from all of this it is clear that:

(1) The early rabbinic commentaries concerning the Messiah *did* fit the picture of Jesus as we have it in the New Testament.

(2) The rabbis formed their own picture of the Messiah that catered to their own political and personal needs.

(3) The rabbis rejected Jesus as the Messiah largely because they couldn't accept the idea of the Incarnation – God and man in One Person, even though their Scriptures and commentaries clearly stated that the Messiah would be far more than a man.

19. Wasn't the Messianic Idea a Christian Invention?

Jesus asked,
> *"What do you think about the Christ [Messiah]?*
> *Whose son is he?"* (Matthew 22:42)

There are some critics who claim that the early Christians, looking for support for their new belief, created a scenario from the Hebrew Scriptures to persuade people Jesus was the divine Messiah. This theory states that, "Even Jesus did not believe he was the Messiah. What we find in Mark is a theory imposed by Mark on the narrative." (119:20; cf. 120:69-71,91)

But it is not possible for the critics to prove their assertions. The idea of a coming Jewish Messiah was not the invention of the Apostles or the early Christian community. Rather, it is beyond dispute that the Messianic promises already existed before Christ appeared on the scene. This can be seen from the following:

1. It can be documented that at the very time of Christ, there was a general expectation among the Jews for their Messiah.

2. As we have already seen, some rabbis before Christ's time understood from the prophecies in Daniel 9:24-27 that the time of the Messiah had to be around the general time of Christ (see our discussion of Daniel 9).

3. History records that there were so many claimants for the title of Messiah during this time. (117:I, 165, IV, 135). (In fact, there was widespread Messianic expectation throughout the East, including in the Sibylline Oracles.) (52:150-153)

4. It is beyond question that the Jews based their Messianic expectation on the prophecies contained in their sacred books. (52:II, 145-153) Gloag has recorded: "It is thus a matter beyond controversy that there existed about the time of our Lord the expectation of the advent of some mighty prince, to whom the Jews gave the name of Messiah. The Jews grounded this expectation on certain prophecies contained in their sacred books." (52:II, 153)

Additional proof that the Jewish people were expecting their Messiah at the time of Christ can be seen in the historical documents of the New Testament. There we find:

(1) It is universally recognized by the "chief priests and teachers of the law" that the Messiah was to be born "in Bethlehem in Judea" on the basis of Micah 5:2 (Mt. 2:4-6).

(2) Godly men such as Simeon were *waiting for the consolation of Israel"* (the Messiah) (Lk. 2:25-26).

(3) The people in general expected the Messiah. *"The people were waiting expectantly and were all wondering in their hearts if John [the Baptist] might possibly be the Christ [Messiah]"* (Lk 3:15).

(4) The Jews of Jerusalem sent priests and Levites to ask John the Baptist as to whether or not he was the Messiah (Jn. 1:19-20).

(5) Crowds of people are pictured arguing as to whether or not Jesus was the Messiah (Jn. 7:40-43).

(6) The Jewish leaders are portrayed as being anxious to have an answer whether or not Jesus was the Messiah (Jn. 10:24).

In conclusion, this evidence clearly indicates that the critics are wrong in asserting the Messianic concept was only a Christian invention.

20. The "Issue" of Interpretation

Many of the Messianic prophecies are clear, but not all of them are. Some of them clearly state they are prophesying about the Messiah. Others appear to intermingle the life events of the prophet who is speaking with the future events that are proclaimed about the Messiah.

Because of this, critics have claimed that the Messianic prophecies are all obscure and their meanings are so vague and ambiguous that their application is doubtful. Here are some of the reasons why Messianic prophecies must be studied carefully (52:II,101-110):

• Sometimes the prophecies are not totally clear by divine appointment. For example, God says the time certain prophecies in Daniel will be fulfilled are *"closed up and sealed until the end of time"* (Dan. 12:8,9; cf. Num. 12:8; Lk. 10:21).

• Sometimes the prophets are given visions in which they see and hear events occurring in the present but which are to be applied to the future. As a result, the appearing of the Messiah is sometimes stated as if it were about to occur immediately, but it is really describing a future event.

• God gives different parts of the total prophetic picture, like various pieces in a puzzle, to His prophets. To one prophet, living in one era, God may reveal information about the Messiah's suffering. To another prophet, living in another time, God may give information about Messiah's birthplace. Because of this, one prophet speaks of the Messiah as the anointed King, another as Jehovah's chosen Servant (Isa. 42:1).

• Sometimes prophetic events are "telescoped" so that the intervening years are deliberately passed over. For example, in Isaiah 52:13-15, first, the Servant of the Lord is portrayed as prosperous, high and lifted up. But then suddenly we are told, ". . . his appearance was so disfigured beyond that of any man and his form marred beyond human likeness."

From the next chapter, Isaiah 53, we realize the Servant must suffer before He prospers.

- Finally, many of the most obscure prophecies are seen to be extremely clear after their fulfillment. For example, in Isaiah 53, the Messiah is portrayed as both the suffering Servant and the conquering King. The text says He will be cut off from the land of the living, but He will also prolong His days. He will be despised and rejected of men, but He will also divide His portion with the great.

From the New Testament, the One who claimed He was the Messiah spoke of His coming to earth a second time. It is *then* we understand fully the information given by the prophets.

The obscurity and seeming contradiction in this Messianic passage has resulted in perplexing many of the rabbis. That's why they tried to solve this perplexing passage by inventing two distinct Messiahs.

But after Jesus, it's obvious that the Messiah was One Person with two different missions. Many prophecies are like this. That is why Gloag and Delitzsch have written, "Such prophecies cannot properly be charged with obscurity: on the contrary, when viewed in the light of their fulfillment, they are plain and obvious." (52:II,107)

Therefore, if some of the Messianic prophecies are obscure, the question is, upon their fulfillment, are they clear and do they point directly to Jesus?

A prophecy that was totally obscure would be one which was so pliable that it could be twisted into finding fulfillment in a thousand different ways. If a statement presents no clear or specific information, such a statement certainly would be meaningless.

Let us illustrate this point by examining an example of a meaningless prophecy. If someone said, "In a future age, when masses accumulate under the sun, a great thing will occur." This would be meaningless. Why? Because each part of this prophecy is either too general or too vague and could have a hundred fulfillments. A future "age" could be any point in the future. "Masses accumulate" could refer to almost anything (people, wealth, clouds, locusts, insects, etc.). "Under the sun" could refer to any event on earth and "a great thing" could be defined in a hundred different ways.

A Messianic prophecy is not like this. It may be brief, terse and initially obscure, but upon careful examination four important facts will be discovered.

(1) *The context limits the meaning*.

Each prophecy is given within an immediate biblical text. This greatly reduces the range of meanings and application of the prophecy. The words in the prophecy are defined and given meaning by the words used in the immediate context.

(2) *The charge of total obscurity is never true*.

Even when partially obscure, the prophecy always gives specific, not generalized, statements. For example, ". . . My servant will prosper, be high and lifted up and greatly exalted . . . his appearance was marred more than any man." Here we can see that the mystery of Isaiah 52:13-14 is cleared up when we realize Isaiah was speaking of Jesus' first coming when He was stricken, smitten and afflicted. Only at Jesus' second coming will verse 13 be fulfilled – "My servant will prosper, be highly lifted up and exalted."

(3) *The partial obscurity itself eventually gives way to clarity*.

The biblical example of Isaiah 53 given above also applies here. The mystery and partial obscurity of Messianic passages have been revealed to be profound and amazing predictions the moment Jesus Christ appeared on the scene.

(4) *The prophetic plan is not yet completed*.

Many prophecies still remain to be fulfilled according to Jesus. When the disciples met Him after His resurrection before He ascended to heaven, they asked Him, *"Lord, are you at this time going to restore the kingdom to Israel?"* He said to them: *"It is not for you to know the times or dates the Father has set by his own authority"* (Acts 1:6,7; cf. 3:21).

Like their fellow countrymen, the disciples were wondering when Jesus would fulfill the Messianic prophecies and institute the Messianic kingdom. Jesus' answer showed it was still future and the Father had set those times and dates by His own authority.

Another example that many prophecies remain to be fulfilled in the future according to Jesus can be seen from His testimony during His trial: *"The high priest said to him, 'I charge you under oath by the living God: tell us if you are the Christ [Messiah], the Son of God.' 'Yes, it is as you say,' Jesus replied. 'But I say to all of you: in the future you will see the Son of Man sitting at the right hand of the Mighty One and coming on the clouds of heaven'"* (Mt. 26:63-64).

This is a direct reference to the greatest Messianic prophecy in the Hebrew Scriptures given by Daniel (Dan. 7:13). It proves Jesus knew He was the Messiah and would at His second coming fulfill what Daniel had said; namely, He would be *"the Son of Man coming on the clouds of heaven"* (Mt. 24:30, 31).

Since Messianic prophecies encompass all the Messiah was to do, and since we know from Jesus that the Messianic program is not yet complete, these prophecies are of necessity not yet completely fulfilled. But there have been enough prophecies fulfilled completely to expect the rest will also be completely fulfilled.

Even a clear and specific prophecy such as Micah 5:2 which predicts the Messiah will be born in Bethlehem Ephrathah, also reveals He will someday be the Ruler over Israel, which is not yet fulfilled.

The different prophecies can be compared to a complex building project that involves the construction of many high-rise buildings, several parks and streams, underground garages, and recreation facilities. One does not evaluate and grade the architect, the workers or the building complex itself when it is only half completed. One can only judge when the complex has been completely finished. Just because part of the foundation and some of the structure is built, this does not mean that the total building will *never* be built. Rather, a good foundation and some of the structure

101

should engender confidence that someday the entire building *will be* built.

Much of what the prophets said has already taken place – the Messiah has been born in Bethlehem, plainly identified Himself as being both God and Messiah (Jn. 4:24-26; Jn. 5:18), suffered and died on the cross for our sins and rose from the dead. On the basis of what has taken place, one may confidently expect that God will bring about the rest.

21. Did the New Testament writers fairly quote the Hebrew Scriptures?

There are some 300 separate, referenced quotations from the Hebrew Scriptures in the New Testament, including a total of 1,300 additional paraphrases and unreferenced quotations. These 1,600 New Testament references refer back to some 1,200 different Hebrew passages. (2:2-3) Dr. Walter Kaiser has correctly stated, "The frequency with which the New Testament writings appeal to the Hebrew Scriptures must be judged by all to be most impressive . . . . The impact of the Hebrew Scriptures on the New Testament will always remain a major consideration in coming to terms with the meaning of the New Testament." (2:225)

The New Testament writers were so convinced that the Hebrew Scriptures had miraculously and clearly predicted the birth, life and death of Jesus Christ that they preached this at the daily risk of losing their lives. History records they eventually *were* martyred because of their belief. Is it reasonable to think they would have died for views of the Messiah that were insufficiently supported by the Hebrew Scriptures? No man gives his life for what is not clear. And certainly, no man gives his life for what he knows is a lie. The prophecies had to be clear, persuasive, and true. They had to point to Jesus alone and not to a hundred other men.

But critics believe the New Testament writers were deceived men who preached a false view of Jesus to the entire world. The critics say the prophecies in the Hebrew Scriptures were never meant to apply to Jesus.

But it was the prophecies themselves that made a strong impression on the disciples. The disciples never would have thought to fabricate a story of Jesus as the Messiah by twisting the Hebrew Scriptures. "How could such a line of reasoning carry any weight, especially with a hostile Jewish audience that was more than skeptical about the illegitimate use of their Scriptures?" (2:229)

Kaiser points out, "The New Testament apostles argue[d] that they [were] finding in the [Hebrew Scriptures] precisely what the original writers understood them to say (e.g., Acts 2:29-34)." (2:230)

Citing Acts 3:19-23, Kaiser argues that "the apostles were so confident of their equating the person, ministry, and office of Jesus with those [Hebrew prophetic] anticipations that they could, at times, threaten their audiences as Peter did on the porch of the temple . . . . The apostles betray no evidence that they were under some compulsion to make the details of the life of Christ fit some predetermined schema forced on the [Hebrew Scriptures] by giving [them] a different sense than what [they] originally had and then building their case on the assumption that the original passage had the same sense they had attributed to it." (2:21-22)

Beecher observes that the historical unity that underlies the New Testament interpretations of the Hebrew Scriptures makes it impossible that the New Testament writers had fabricated the picture of Jesus. He concludes that the biblical authors are in a class by themselves and that even the best historians of our own time do not surpass them:

> "Their interfitting and continuity is proof that they are true to reality; for chance statement would not fit thus, and it is unimaginable that all these writers joined in fabricating a fiction. There are arguments from the character of the biblical men. The loftiness of their point of view is wonderful. If we account for it by their inspiration, we have in it direct proof of the divine authority of the men and of their writings. If we try to account for it otherwise, we have to attribute to them remarkable insight and rare trustworthiness, and we thus put ourselves under obligation to accept their testimony, both in regard to the history they narrate and when they claim divine authority for themselves." (3:409-410)

Other scholars have also agreed with Beecher's conclusion: "The great bulk of the [New Testament] quotations are careful reproductions or translations of the original Scripture. In most instances the historical sense is carefully preserved, and often the source of the quotation is accurately acknowledged even though such reference was not the normal practice at that time." (in 2:228)

Careful examination of the evidence (comparing the New Testament passages quoting Hebrew passages) reveals there can be no doubt that the New Testament writers fairly quoted the Hebrew Scriptures.

22. Modern Jewish Views on Messianic Passages

Modern Orthodox Judaism denies that Jesus is the Jewish Messiah. World famous Orthodox Jewish theologian Pinchas Lapide and Ulrich Luz have set forth the statements of some who have asserted that Jesus is not the Messiah in their book *Jesus in Two Perspectives: A Jewish-Christian Dialogue*. After each statement we will give a brief response.

OBJECTION:

(1) "Eduard Schweizer writes: 'Argument has waged for decades over whether he himself thought he was the Messiah . . . . Nevertheless, there is not a single genuine saying of Jesus in which he refers to himself as the Messiah.'" (10:46)

Yet in John 4:25-26 anybody can read: *"The woman said, 'I know the Messiah (called Christ) is coming. When he comes, he will explain everything to us.' Then Jesus declared, 'I who speak to you am he.'"*

This is not the only place where Jesus refers to Himself as the Messiah. At His trial, He was asked by the high priest, *" 'Are you the Christ, the Son of the Blessed One?'" 'I am,' said Jesus. 'And you will see the Son of Man sitting on the right hand of the Mighty One and coming on the clouds of heaven.'*

"The high priest tore his clothes. 'Why do we need any more witnesses?'" he asked. 'You have heard the blasphemy. What do you think?' They all condemned him as worthy of death" (Mk. 14:61-64).

World renowned trial attorney in America and Great Britain, John Warwick Montgomery, in examining the circumstances surrounding Jesus' trial, has declared, "Although not much good can be said about the high priest at this kangaroo court, one thing is certain: he correctly recognized that Jesus was claiming to be no less than God Incarnate, and that if he was not what he claimed, then he was a blasphemer." (118:54)

OBJECTION:

(2) ". . . It has been established historically that 'only later was

Isaiah 53 associated with the Messiah.' 'Actually
the thought of a suffering Messiah was completely
remote from the synagogue of Jesus' time.'"
(10:30)

Such early rabbis as the great Maimonides and Crispin might
disagree with the above statement concerning Isaiah 53. They said,
"[Isaiah 53] was given of God as a description of the Messiah,
whereby, when any should claim to be the Messiah, to judge by the
resemblance or non-resemblance to it whether he were the Messiah
or no' . . . .[Crispin also said that those who apply the passage to
Israel have "forsaken the knowledge of our teachers, and inclined
after the stubbornness or their own hearts and of their own opinions.
(55:228)]" (Ellison says the suffering Messiah concept cannot be
traced earlier that 150 A.D., but see p. 26 note)

Another rabbi, R. Elyyah de Vidas, says, 'The meaning of "he
was wounded for our transgressions, . . . bruised for our iniquities" is, that since the Messiah bears our iniquities, which
produce the effect of His being bruised, it follows that whoso will
not admit that the Messiah thus suffers for our iniquities must
endure and suffer for them himself.'" (55:225-229) (See our
discussion of Isaiah 53 on pages 39-51.)

OBJECTION:

(3) "For Jewish scholars the evidence of the resurrection was
not a proof of Jesus' Messiahship, because for them
the idea of resurrection was not connected with the
Messianic expectation of salvation." (10:31)

But Isaiah 53:10-11, without specifically using the word resurrection, certainly calls for it.

Also, David prophesied of the Messiah in Psalm 62:10 and 49:9
that, *"Because you will not abandon me to the grave, nor will you
let your Holy One see decay"* (Ps. 16:10, cf. Acts 2:27-31;
13:34-37).

And finally, if Jesus actually did resurrect from the dead and
offered this as proof for His claims to be God (see Appendix One),
then such a miracle would prove He was God whether or not Jewish

scholars held the idea previously. In other words, just because someone has never considered the idea of a man resurrecting from the dead, when it happens, to ignore it because you had not thought of the idea first would be ridiculous.

OBJECTION:

(4) ". . . Jesus never revealed himself publicly as the Messiah, and strictly forbade others to describe him as such." (10:39)

Such a statement insults people who have read Jesus' statements where He plainly said He was the Messiah.

OBJECTION:

(5) (Concerning certain political prophecies of the Messiah) "Jesus of Nazareth did not fulfill any of these expectations – nor did he ever promise to fulfill them." (10:29)

To say Jesus never promised to fulfill prophecies connected to the political realm cannot be taken seriously in light of what He told the Jewish high priest at His trial, *I am [the Christ]; and you will see the Son of Man sitting on the right hand of power and coming with the clouds of heaven"* (Mk. 14:62). The expression "Son of Man" is a direct quote from Daniel 7. "[It] is really one of the loftiest ascriptions given to God's Messiah in the Old Testament." (118:54) An even stronger promise of Jesus concerning His return to rule the world can be seen in Matthew 24:27-31; 25:31-33.

OBJECTION:

Genesis 3:15 – "Yet there is absolutely no proof to assume that this verse is messianic or that the Messiah is to be born in a supernatural way." (54:3)

How can anyone make such a statement when proof can easily be found in the pre-Christian Septuagint translation of the Hebrew Scriptures? (See our discussion of Genesis 3:15 on pages 22-26.)

As Dr. Kaiser has written, "But you may say, 'Are you sure that anyone ever had this idea before the Christian century?' Yes. There is an article that appeared in the 1965 issue of the *Journal of Biblical Literature* . . . . written by Ralph Martin. It deals with the earliest pre-Christian interpretation of Genesis 3:15, which could be demonstrated. He took the Septuagint rendering of this text (the Septuagint comes from the 3rd century B.C.) and "demonstrated beyond a shadow of a doubt, on philological grounds, that the Jewish community – at least the one in Alexandria – understood this to be Messianic and this well in advance of the birth of Christ." (81; cf. 1:42; 2:42)

OBJECTION:

Deuteronomy 18:15, 18 – "It is claimed by Christian missionaries that the verses constitute a prophetic reference to Jesus. There is absolutely no truth to this contention." (54:17)

If so, why is it that the apostles and the early Christians all used this quote without explanation and assumed their Jewish audience knew what they were talking about? Stephen used this prophecy in Acts 7:37 and Peter used it in Acts 3:22. (See our discussion of this verse on pages 31-34.)

OBJECTION:

Isaiah 52:13 – 53:12 – "What Jews find even more amazing and mystifying is how any person who studies this chapter critically can possibly believe it alludes to Jesus . . . . Isaiah 53 speaks of the nation of Israel, ..." (54:36)

The great rabbis Maimonides and Crispin, as we have already seen, specifically state that this passage does *not* speak of the *nation* of Israel but it *does* refer to the Messiah.

To see if this passage does fit Jesus, see our chapter on Isaiah 53.

OBJECTION:

Micah 5:1 – "This verse refers to the Messiah, a descendant of David . . . . The text does not necessarily mean the Messiah will be born in that

town, but that his family originates from there
. . . . In any case, being born in Bethlehem is of
dubious value in establishing messianic creden-
tials for Jesus." (54:76-77)

No one can know the meaning of the text except from the words
in the text, and the biblical text plainly says the *Messiah* will be
born in Bethlehem, not his family.

It's amazing that anyone would make the above statement when
it is clear from the historical background in the New Testament, that
the chief priests and teachers of the law advised Herod that
according to the verse, the Messiah would be born in Bethlehem.
Magi (wisemen) asked King Herod, " *'Where is the one that has
been born King of the Jews? We saw his star in the East and have
come to worship him.' When King Herod heard this, he was
disturbed, and all Jerusalem with him. When he had called together
all the peoples, chief priests and teachers of the law, he asked them
where the Christ was to be born. 'In Bethlehem in Judea,' they
replied, 'for this is what the prophet has written . . .'"* (Mt. 2:1-5).
(Also see our discussion on Micah 5:2.)

OBJECTION:

Zechariah 12:10 – "Of course, God cannot literally be pierced." (54:80)

The problem with this objection is that in the text that is exactly
what God did say: *"They [Israel] will look on Me whom they have
pierced."* The only way to get around this statement is to change
the plain meaning of the words.

If God takes upon Himself a human nature and becomes a man in
the Incarnation, then, if anyone pierced or crucified that man, it
would be correct to say they "have pierced or crucified" God.
Jesus claimed He was God and was crucified. But remember,
because Christ was full humanity and full Deity, when His human
nature died, His divine nature, which could not cease, continued to
live and reside fully in Jesus' body. When Jesus rose bodily from
the grave, Jesus was again full humanity and full Deity in One
Person.

OBJECTION:

Psalms 22 – "The early Christians, in interpreting and expanding the accounts of Jesus' death, sought confirmation of their claims in the Hebrew Scriptures. Believing Jesus to be the fulfillment of biblical prophecy, they proclaimed him the Messiah. The Scriptures were searched for evidence which could be used to demonstrate the truth of their hypothesis. This was especially true for the crucifixion . . . . [But] Psalms 22 cannot be made to apply to the life of Jesus." (54:95, 97)

One only needs to read Psalm 22 to see whether or not this description fits Jesus' suffering. It's not a matter of making it apply; rather, it is a matter of whether it does apply.

23. How the Early Jews Who Believed on Jesus Proved That He Was the Jewish Messiah

The Gospels comprise four books written by Jewish people who knew Jesus personally for over three years. All of the writers claimed their books were based on firsthand testimony of those who were witnesses of Jesus' life. Because of this, these authors were qualified to ascertain whether or not Jesus really did fit the facts predicted about the Messiah.

We should remember that the most powerful and persuasive testimony that Jesus was the Messiah was written by Jews. In fact, the entire New Testament was written by Jews (although, according to tradition, Luke was a Greek).

Today, Christians are only following the testimony of the earliest Jewish converts that Jesus was in fact the Messiah. What is presumptuous is for anyone 2,000 years after the facts to think they know more than the eyewitnesses and state Jesus could not be the Messiah without even considering the evidence.

It is true that not all of the Jews during Jesus' time accepted Him as the Messiah. Because of this, there are some today who claim there is no reason why anyone ought to believe Jesus was the Messiah. But such persons have a hard time explaining why literally thousands of Jews *did* accept Jesus as their Messiah (Acts 21:20). Not only is it hard to explain why this happened in Israel during that time, but why it continues to happen all over the world today (Acts 2:15-16, 32, 36-41; 4:2-4; cf. 74:23,24; 75:120).

Certainly the evidence must have been persuasive to convince so many Jews and Gentiles all over the world that Jesus alone, among the scores of other claimants, was the Messiah.

What is even more remarkable is that the Jewish writers of the Gospels proved that Jesus was the Messiah on the basis of the Hebrew Scriptures and thousands of other Jews believed them. The only reason the early Jewish converts were successful in persuading other Jews to believe in Jesus was because (1) the prophecies were clearly present in the Hebrew Scriptures and (2) because only Jesus fulfilled them.

112

Here are a few examples of how often the early Jewish converts appealed to the prophecies from the Hebrew Scriptures as recorded in the book of Acts:

(1) In Acts 2:22-37 at Pentecost, the Apostle Peter quotes the Messianic prophecies in Psalm 16 and Psalm 110. He cites Psalm 16 as proof of Christ's resurrection, reasoning that since King David died and his body did see corruption, the last part of the Psalm could not fully apply to David. It applied to Christ. Peter explained, *"Seeing what was ahead, he [David] spoke of the resurrection of the Christ [Messiah], that he was not abandoned to the grave, nor did his body see decay"* (Acts 2:31).

Peter quoted Psalm 110 where it says the Messiah was not only David's son, but his Lord and predicts the Messiah will ascend to sit at God's right hand (God says to him, *"Sit at my right hand"*). Peter concludes, *"Therefore let all Israel be assured of this: God has made this Jesus, whom you crucified, both Lord and Christ [Messiah]"* (Acts 2:36).

(2) In Acts Chapter 3, Deuteronomy 18:15-19, Genesis 12:3, and Isaiah 52 are quoted. In referring to these Hebrew passages as Messianic prophecies, the apostle shows he believes Jesus is (A) "the prophet like Moses" in Deuteronomy 18; (B) the promise to Abraham that through him all people on earth would be blessed in Genesis 12; and (C) the "Servant" of God in Isaiah 52. He concludes by saying:

> *"But this is how God fulfilled what He had foretold through all the prophets, saying that His Christ [Messiah] would suffer . . . . Indeed, all the prophets from Samuel on, as many as have spoken, have foretold **these days**. And you are heirs of the prophets and of the covenant God made with your fathers"* (Acts 3:18, 24,25, emphasis added).

(3) In Acts 10:43, we find the Hebrew Scriptures cited in the statement: "All the prophets testify about Him [Jesus the Messiah]. That everyone who believes in Him receives forgiveness of sins through His name."

113

(4) In Acts 13:23-41, the Apostle Paul explains to his listeners that Jesus is the Messiah using the Messianic prophecies found in 2 Samuel 7, Psalms 2, Psalms 16 and Habakkuk 1:5. Paul is convinced that *"in condemning Him [Jesus] they fulfilled the words of the prophets that are read every Sabbath"* (Acts 13:27). But he is also convinced the Hebrew Scriptures offer hope: *"What God promised our fathers, He has fulfilled for us, their children, by raising up Jesus"* (Acts 13:32); further, *"God has brought to Israel the Savior Jesus, as He promised"* (Acts 13:23).

There are many more examples that could be given. But from these it can be seen that the constant appeal of the Jewish Christians in the New Testament was to what "the prophets" had spoken about the Messiah. Because Jesus fulfilled many incredibly precise prophecies the prophets had spoken and because Jesus promised to return and fulfill all the rest (Acts 3:21; Mt. 24:30; 25:31-33), He had to be the Messiah. This is the only reason why so many Jews accepted Jesus as their Messiah. The following passages further document and show this was so. (Emphasis added by the authors.)

(5) Acts 14:1 – *"At Iconium Paul and Barnabas went as usual **into the Jewish Synagogue**. There they spoke so effectively that a great number of Jews and Gentiles believed."*

(6) Acts 17:2-3 – *"As his custom was, Paul went into **the Synagogue**, and on three Sabbath days **he reasoned with them from the Scriptures**, explaining and proving that **the Christ [Messiah] had to suffer and rise from the dead**. 'This Jesus I am proclaiming to you is the Christ,' He said. Some of the Jews were persuaded . . . ."*

(7) Acts 17:10-12 – *"[Paul and Silas] went to **the Jewish Synagogue**. Now the Bereans were of more noble character than the Thessalonicans, for they received the message with great eagerness and **examined the Scriptures every day** to see if what Paul said was true. [As a result] many of **the Jews believed**, as did also a number of prominent Greek women and many Greek men."*

(8) Acts 18:4-5 – *"Every Sabbath he [Paul] reasoned in the Synagogue, trying to persuade Jews and Greeks . . . . Paul*

devoted himself exclusively to preaching, testifying to the Jews *that Jesus was the Christ [Messiah].''*

(9) Acts 18:28 – *"[Apollos] vigorously refuted the Jews in public debate, **proving from the Scriptures that Jesus was the Christ** [Messiah].''*

(10) Acts 26:22-23,27 – *"But I [Paul] have had God's help to this very day, and so I stand here and testify to small and great alike. I am saying nothing beyond what the **prophets and Moses said** would happen – **that the Christ [Messiah] would suffer** and, as the first to rise from the dead, would proclaim light to His own people and to the Gentiles . . . . King Agrippa, **do you believe the prophets**? I know you do.''*

It is apparent that thousands of Jews (Acts 21:20) accepted Jesus as their Messiah solely on the basis of the Hebrew Scriptures. The brightest Jewish minds of the day could not dissuade them otherwise. Simply put, these new Jewish converts firmly believed that the Scriptures had been fulfilled in Jesus. In fact, because of the scriptural prophecies, even many of the Jewish leaders came to believe Jesus was the Messiah (Jn. 7:48; 12:42).

24. If Jesus Is the Messiah, What Should You Do?

The evidence in the Hebrew Scriptures shows that Jesus is the Messiah. God gave this evidence hundreds of years in advance so you would be certain to identify Him. But Jesus, who *is* the Messiah, desires for you to know Him personally, not just for you to know facts about Him intellectually. He has told us how that can happen, what He is willing to do, and what we must do.

First, as Isaiah said, *"All of us, like sheep, have gone astray, each of us has turned to his own way"* (Isa. 53:6). God says we are sinners and we must admit this to Him.

Second, besides admitting to God that we are sinners, we must realize the precarious position we are in. God says, *"Your iniquities have made a separation between you and your God, and your sins have hid His face from you, so that He does not hear"* (Isa. 59:2). God told the prophet Ezekiel, *"The soul who sins is the one who will die"* (Ezek. 18:4).

We all realize we are sinners and are uncomfortable with the idea of death and standing before God to be judged for our actions. Jesus taught that all judgment was in His hands (Jn. 5:22,23), and that He alone would decide the eternal destiny of every man, woman and child who ever lived (Mt. 25:31-46; Jn. 5:21-29).

If all of our life we ignore God, keep Him out of our life, and hold onto our sinful ways, at the Judgment the prophet Daniel teaches that the *"multitudes who sleep in the dust of the earth will awake: some to everlasting life, others to shame and everlasting contempt"* (Dan. 12:2).

Jesus the Messiah said the same thing, *"They [unrepentant persons] will go away to eternal punishment, but the righteous [those forgiven of their sins] into eternal life"* (Mt. 25:46).

Third, God wants us to recognize His Messiah *paid* for our sins by His atoning death on the cross. Isaiah explained long ago, *"The Lord has laid on him [the Messiah] the iniquity of us all"* (Isa. 53:6). *"He was pierced for our transgressions, he was crushed for*

116

our iniquities; the punishment that brought us peace was upon him'' (Isa. 53:5). *"He poured out his life unto death and was numbered with the transgressors. For he bore the sins of many . . .''* (Isa. 53:12). *"For Christ [the Messiah] died for sins once for all, the righteous for the unrighteous, to bring you to God''* (1 Pet. 3:18).

The primary reason Jesus said He came into the world was to rescue from divine judgment those who were sinners (Jn. 3:16,17). He promised men they could have their sins fully and freely forgiven if they believed on Him (Jn. 3:16,17; 6:47; cf. Eph. 2:8,9).

Fourth, God asks us to call to the Messiah and ask Him to forgive us our sins: *"Seek the Lord while he may be found; call on him while he is near. Let the wicked forsake his way and the evil man his thoughts. Let him turn to the Lord, and he will have mercy on him, and to our God, for he will freely pardon''* (Isa. 55:6, 7).

The Messiah fulfilled Isaiah 53 by paying the divine penalty for our sins. By trusting in Him personally, we can have forgiveness of our sins and enter into a new relationship with God. He promises to give us life with Him forever.

Jesus the Messiah promises, *"Truly, truly I say to you, he who hears my word and believes him who sent me has eternal life, and does not come into judgment but is passed out of death into life''* (Jn. 5:24). And He promises, *"This is eternal life, that they may know thee, the only true God and Jesus Christ whom thou hast sent''* (Jn. 17:3).

In the Hebrew Scriptures, Jeremiah prophesied, *"Behold the days come, says Jehovah, that I will raise to David a righteous Branch . . . and this is his name by which he shall be called, Jehovah **our righteousness**''* (Jer. 23:5, 6). This was fulfilled in Jesus. How? The Apostle Paul explains how God imparts a righteous standing (because of Jesus' death on the cross) to every sinner who will place his faith in Him.

> *"But now a righteousness from God, apart from law, has been made known, to which the Law and the Prophets testify. This righteousness from God*

117

comes through faith in Jesus Christ to all who believe. There is no difference [between Jew and Gentile], for all have sinned and fall short of the glory of God, and [both] are justified freely by his grace through the redemption that came by Christ [Messiah] Jesus. God presented him as a sacrifice of atonement, . . .'' (Rom. 3:21-25).

Not only does God provide for us a righteous standing before Him, but God is also adamant that our coming to know Him will not be based on our works, on anything that we do. It is based on what Christ did for us. The way we can accept God's great gift He offers is by placing our faith, simply trusting in what God promises. Abraham is an example of one having faith in God's promise:

"If, in fact, Abraham was justified by works, he had something to boast about — but not before God. What does the Scripture say? 'Abraham believed God, and it was credited to him as righteousness.' Now when a man works, his wages are not credited to him as a gift, but as an obligation. However, to the man who does not work [for salvation], but trusts God who justifies the wicked, his faith is credited as righteousness. David says the same thing when he speaks of the blessedness of the men to whom God credits righteousness apart from works: . . .'' (Rom. 4:2-6).

So, right now, do you understand that God sees your sin as something very serious? Do you understand He sent His own Son to die on the cross for you? God says He knows all about your sins, and says they separate you from Him. But He loves you. He desires that you would find life in Him, not death because of ignoring His free gift. He has already sent His Messiah to atone for your sins. On the basis of that atonement, He now invites you to turn to Him and accept the gift Jesus provided.

To receive Jesus as your Messiah, your Lord and Savior right now, you may pray a prayer like the following:

"Dear God, I ask Jesus, your Messiah, to enter my life and be my Lord and Savior. I recognize that you have dealt with my sins when Jesus died on the cross. I acknowledge my sins and ask you to forgive me. From this moment on I believe Jesus is the Messiah and He died on the cross for me. I believe He rose from the dead and is living now, and I place all of my faith and trust in Him to be my Lord and Savior and to give me His eternal life. Please show me the next steps of how to follow You."

If you have received Jesus as your Messiah and Savior, please write to us here at The John Ankerberg Show. Let us know you have made this decision. In return we will send you some helpful information on how to live your new spiritual life and grow in the grace and knowledge of God (2 Pet. 3:18).

APPENDIX ONE

Did Jesus Christ Really Rise from the Dead?

"Of [the many] Messianic claimants, only one, Jesus of Nazareth, so impressed his disciples that he became their Messiah. And he did so after the very crucifixion which should have refuted his claims decisively. . .It was not Jesus' life [alone] which proved beyond question that he was the Messiah, the Christ. It was his resurrection. It was only when his disciples were convinced that Jesus had indeed risen from the dead that they were stunned into awareness that Jesus was the Christ."(18:62)

If Jesus Christ did, in fact, rise from the dead, then one must accept the claims about Himself as being true — that He was in fact God Incarnate (Jn. 5:18; 19:7; Rom. 1:3). No one else of an estimated 100 billion persons who have ever lived in human history has ever risen from the dead. He predicted in advance He would rise from the dead (on several occasions — Mt. 16:21; 26:32; Mk. 14:28; Lk. 9:22; Jn. 2:19) and then proceeded to do just that.

Some individuals have tried to make similar predictions about coming back from the dead throughout history, such as "Father Divine," but in the end they all have been proven liars. Only Jesus Christ conquered death and offered His resurrection as verifiable proof, validating His claim to be God Incarnate.

Even the skeptics of this world believe Jesus Christ stands as a symbol of truth and integrity. But if He was such a man, how could He make such incredible claims about Himself unless they were true? He could only make these claims for Himself if He was telling the truth and if He knew that He was the Jewish Messiah, the God-Man, the Savior of the world.

Right here, Dr. Pinchas Lapide, a Jewish scholar, has a logical problem in his consideration of Jesus. He says he accepts Jesus' bodily resurrection "as a historical event" and "a fact of history."(70:7, 126-131) But after admitting Jesus rose from the dead, and after admitting this was a true miracle of God, Dr. Lapide rejects Jesus as being the Messiah of the Jews. How can Dr. Lapide know more about the significance of the resurrection than Jesus Himself who said this showed He was the Messiah and truly God? How do we know the resurrection really occurred?

> (1) On the basis of accepted principles of historic and textual analysis, the New Testament documents are shown to be reliable and trustworthy historical documents. That is, they give accurate (eyewitness) primary source evidence for the life and death of Jesus Christ. In fact, in 2,000 years the New Testament authors have never been proven unethical, dishonest, or to have been deceived.

> (2) In these historical records, Jesus clearly claims to be God Incarnate (Jn. 5:18; 10:27-33); exercises innumerable divine prerogatives; and rests His claims on His miracles (Jn. 10:37-38; 11:43-45), His greatest miracle being His literal physical resurrection from the dead (Jn. 10:17-18).

> (3) In each of the Gospels, Christ's resurrection is minutely described, and for 2,000 years it has been incapable of disproof despite the detailed scholarship of the world's best skeptics. The simple truth is that the historic fact of the resurrection proves Jesus' claim to Deity.(68; cf. 113:138-139; 114:248-260)

The resurrection cannot be rejected on anti-supernaturalist grounds. Miracles are impossible only if one knows in advance that they have never happened. But the only way anyone can know that is by first examining the evidence. The probability of a miracle is determined by the cumulative weight of the evidence, not philosophical bias.

On the basis of internal, external, and bibliographic data, one may establish beyond all doubt that the Gospels are reliable primary source material. The *internal* evidence proves that the writers were neither deceived nor deceivers. The *external* evidence (evidence lying outside the New Testament itself) also points clearly to the truthfulness of the accounts and the factualness of the resurrection of Christ (see quote below).

The *bibliographic* evidence proves that the content found in these documents is reliable and accurate.(121:135-85; 33:39-53) This is why it is a historical fact that Jesus Christ taught and lived what the New Testament says He taught.

We have over 5,300 extant Greek manuscript portions or manuscripts of the New Testament, over 10,000 Latin Vulgate plus 9,300 other versions as well as 36,000 early (100 to 300 A.D.) patristic quotations of the New Testament. In fact, if the documents we now possess of the New Testament were lost, we could reconstruct the entire New Testament (except 11 verses) from the writings of the Church Fathers.(121:33:39-53; 121:359)

Given the fact that the early extant Greek manuscripts (the papyrii and early uncials) date much closer to the originals than any other documents of ancient literature, and with the overwhelming abundance of manuscript attestation, any doubt as to the integrity or authenticity of the New Testament text has been removed.(121:39-46; cf. 121)

In fact, this is the accepted consensus of biblical scholarship in general. This wealth of manuscript material has led such scholars as Wescott and Hort, Ezra Abbot, Philip Shaff, A. T. Robertson and Geisler and Nix to place the restoration of the original text at 99 percent.(121:238,239; 365-367) They have concluded that no other document of the ancient period is as well attested as the Gospels, and if their reliability is rejected, then all the works of ancient antiquity must be rejected on the same basis. But such skepticism is not seen concerning other works.

In examining the Gospels, it is an accepted standard of historical analysis to assume the truth of an author of a document unless fraud or error disqualifies the writer. Examining the trustworthiness of the Gospels, one finds extreme care was exercised by the writers (Lk. 1:1-3), there are numerous claims to eyewitness testimony (Jn. 19:35; 1 Jn. 1:3; Acts 2:22; 26:24-26; 2 Pet. 1:16, etc.) and there is no error or contradiction in their writing. This shows the New Testament authors can be trusted.

In examining the ancient documents outside the New Testament (the external evidence) Professor of Philosophy Dr. G. R. Habermas in his *Ancient Evidence for the Life of Jesus* observes,

> "Using only the information gleaned from these ancient extrabiblical sources, what can we conclude concerning the death and resurrection of Jesus?. . . . Of the seventeen documents examined in this chapter, eleven different works speak of the death of Jesus in varying amounts of detail, with five of these specifying crucifixion as the mode. . . . It is this author's view that the death of Jesus by crucifixion can be asserted as a historical fact from this data. . . . The ancient references to the resurrection are fewer and more questionable. Of the seventeen sources, only six either imply or report this occurrence, with four of these works being questioned in our study. . . . [Can] the empty tomb. . .be established as historical by this extrabiblical evidence alone[?] There are some strong considerations in its favor. First, the Jewish sources which we have examined admit the empty tomb, thereby providing evidence from hostile documents. . . . Second, there are apparently no ancient sources which assert that the tomb still contained Jesus' body. While such an argument from silence does not prove anything, it is made stronger by the first consideration from the hostile

sources and further complements it. Third, our study has shown that Jesus taught in Palestine and was crucified and buried in Jerusalem under Pontius Pilate. These sources assert that Christianity had its beginnings in the same location. But could Christianity have survived in this location, based on its central claim that Jesus was raised from the dead, if the tomb had not been empty? It must be remembered that the resurrection of the body was a predominant view of first century Jews. To declare a bodily resurrection if the body was still in a nearby tomb points out the dilemma here. Of all places, evidence was readily available in Jerusalem to disprove this central tenet of Christian belief. The Jewish leaders had both a motive and the means to get such evidence if it was available.''(69:112-113)

In his excellent study *The Son Rises*, Philosophy of Religion Professor Dr. William Lane Craig, on the basis of the historical evidence in the documents, has concluded that literally every attempt to explain the resurrection of Jesus on the basis of other theories outside the New Testament fails. Indeed, these theories are actually more difficult to believe than the resurrection itself.

Craig shows ten converging lines of historical evidence support the fact that Jesus' tomb was found empty and that no natural explanation could account for this.(68:45-91)

Next, he shows that there are four converging lines of historical evidence that support the fact, that on various occasions and at different places, Jesus appeared bodily and physically alive from the dead to many witnesses. Again, no natural explanation could account for these appearances.(68:91-127)

Third, Craig points out that the very origin of the Christian faith depends completely on the fact of Jesus' resurrection.(68:127-135) Christianity would never have begun, nor could it have continued, if the resurrection were not true. In summary, "Each of these three great facts, the empty tomb, the appearances, the origin of the Christian faith — is independently established. Together they point with unwavering conviction to the same unavoidable and marvelous conclusion: *Jesus actually rose from the dead*."(68:134)

But is the evidence in the New Testament the kind that would stand up in the real world — evidence that would stand up in a court of law and be conclusive enough to convict someone? Many of the great minds of legal history (Hugo Grotius, Simon Greenleaf, Edmund Bennett,(123) Irwin Linton, etc.) and of today, Lord Chancellor Hailsham,(122) Sir Norman Anderson,(124) Jacques Ellul and John Warwick Montgomery(118) have, on the grounds of strict legal evidence, accepted the Gospels as straightforward history. Because of the facts, they have also been compelled to believe in the resurrection of Christ.

Now, lawyers are known for their expertise in investigating the evidence — indeed, for them, the evidence is everything. It is not by mistake that Hugo Grotius, "the father of international law," wrote *The Truth of the Christian Religion* (1627). The greatest authority on English and American common law evidence in the nineteenth century was Harvard Law School Professor Simon Greenleaf. After being challenged by his students to apply the laws of legal evidence to the Gospel accounts, he wrote *Testimony of the Evangelists* in which he concluded the resurrection of Christ did happen. Edmund H. Bennett (1824-1898) was for over 20 years the dean of the Boston University Law School. He wrote *The Four Gospels from a Lawyer's Standpoint* (1899) and concluded they were truthful accounts, including when they spoke of the resurrection of Christ from the dead. Irwin Linton had represented cases before the Supreme Court and wrote *A Lawyer Examines the Bible* (1943, 1977). In this book he stated:

> "So invariable had been my observation that
> he who does not accept wholeheartedly the

evangelical, conservative belief in Christ and the scriptures has never read, has forgotten, or never been able to weigh — and certainly is utterly unable to refute — the irresistible force of the cumulative evidence upon which such faith rests, that there seems ample ground for the conclusion that such ignorance is an invariable element in such belief.''(112:45)

There can be no doubt that the men just noted are well acquainted with legal reasoning and the nature of evidence. They *all* concluded the writers of the New Testament were reliable and telling the truth. They *all* agreed that on the basis of legal evidence, no jury in the world would fail to bring in a positive verdict for the resurrection of Christ.

The point is this: if the evidence shows that Christ rose from the dead, then He is both God and Messiah, just as He claimed.

APPENDIX TWO

What Was the Length of a Year in Daniel 9?

As we have already seen, the "weeks" are "years." But what is the length of the year? How many days?

The calendar year used in the Scriptures must be determined from the Scriptures themselves. We will show why Daniel's figures were based on a year of 360 days.

In the Scriptures we find a historical example in Genesis 7. Comparing Genesis 7:11 with Genesis 8:4 and the two of these with Genesis 7:24 and Genesis 8:3, it is apparent that the flood began on the seventeenth day of the *second month* and came to an end on the seventeenth day of the *seventh month*, a period of exactly *five months*.

Then in Genesis 8:3, the length of the five-month period is given in days, and it is stated to be exactly "150 days." Dividing 150 days by five months leads to the conclusion that thirty days was the length of a month. Twelve such months would be a 360-day year.

The second example is found in the prophetical passages of Daniel and Revelation. As we have already seen, a "week" in Daniel 9 stood for a period of seven years. In Daniel 9:27 a future persecution is said to begin in the "middle" of the seventieth *week*. Obviously, the middle of a week (a seven-year period of time) is three and one-half years.

Two chapters earlier in Daniel 7:24-25, the same persecution is spoken of. There the duration of persecution is also given as "a time, times, and half a time," or three and a half years.

Then, Revelation 13:4-7 speaks of the same future persecution lasting "forty and two months." Forty-two months is exactly three and a half years.

Finally, Revelation 12:13,14 refers to the same event, and states the duration of time in the exact same words used in Daniel

7:25 — "a time, and times, and half a time." In Revelation 12:6 this period is given an exact number of *days* – one thousand two hundred and sixty *days* which is exactly three and a half years or forty-two months.

Therefore, it is clear that the number of days in a year used by Daniel in the seventy-weeks prophecy is fixed by Scripture itself as exactly 360 days.

The Church Father Jerome, writing in 406-408 A.D., agreed. He acknowledged that "the Hebrews,. . .did not number their months according to the movement of the sun [365 days], but rather according to the moon [360 days].''(104:97) (Israel had various methods of intercalating [adjusting] their 360 days so the year would come out correctly with a solar year. A 360-day year is strange to our ears, but it was the common calendar of those times.[17:136])

Thus, from the decree of Artaxerxes in 444 B.C. until after the 69th week, 483 years later, when Gabriel announced the Messiah would be killed in Jerusalem — we discover this turns out to be the very time in which Christ Himself lived.

Professor Harold W. Hoehner, in his *Chronological Aspects of the Life of Christ* explains in detail the calculations:

"Using the [accepted] 360-day [lunar] year the calculation would be as follows. Multiplying the 69 weeks by seven years for each week by 360 days gives a total of 173,880 days. The difference between 444 B.C. and A.D. 33, then, is 476 solar years. By multiplying 476 by 365.24219879 or by 365 days, 5 hours, 48 minutes, 45.975 seconds, one comes to 173,855.28662404 days or 173,855 days, 6 hours, 52 minutes, 44 seconds. This leaves only 25 days to be accounted for between 444 B.C. and A.D. 33. By adding the 25 days to March 5 (of 444 B.C.), one comes to March 30 (of A.D. 33) which was Nisan 10 [Jewish calendar] in

128

A.D. 33. This is the triumphal entry of Jesus into Jerusalem. . . . As predicted in Zechariah 9:9, Christ presented himself to Israel as Messiah the King for the last time and the multitude of the disciples shouted loudly by quoting from a Messianic psalm: 'Blessed is the King who comes in the name of the Lord' (Ps. 118:26; Mt. 21:9; Mk. 11:10; Lk. 19:38; Jn. 12:13). This occurred on Monday, Nisan 10 (March 30) and only four days later on Friday, Nisan 14, April 3rd, A.D. 33, Jesus was cut off or crucified.''(17:138-139)

APPENDIX THREE

Dr. Walter Kaiser, Jr. is one of the leading theologians and biblical scholars on the Hebrew Scriptures in America today. He is Professor of Semitic Languages and Old Testament and Dean of Trinity Evangelical Divinity School.

In the following appendix, Dr. Kaiser discusses the important Messianic prophecy of Isaiah 7:14 – Would the Messiah be "virgin born"?

Dr. Walter Kaiser, Jr. gave this paper at "The Ritter Lecture for 1987." It was delivered at the Evangelical School of Theology in Myerstown, Pennsylvania.

The Promise of Isaiah 7:14 and the Single-Meaning Hermeneutic [INTERPRETATION]

"Probably no single passage of the Old Testament has been so variously interpreted or has given rise to so much controversy as the prophecy contained in these verses (surrounding Isaiah 7:14)."[1]

Almost every interpreter of this text echoes a similar conclusion; in fact, so divergent are the views and so intractable are the component parts of the historical events that make up the background for this text that Brevard S. Childs opined, "It seems unlikely that a satisfactory historical solution will be forthcoming *without fresh* extra-biblical evidence."[2]

I. The Hermeneutical Issues

But the most severe problem of all revolves around the chronological data pertaining to the birth, reign and the northern Israel and Assyrian synchronisms of the Judean King Hezekiah. H. H. Rowley, that nestor of Old Testament bibliography, exclaimed: "This is one of the most tangled problems of the chronology of the monarchy, and an extraordinary variety of dates for the reign of Hezekiah will be found amongst scholars."[3]

As if all of this were not enough to exacerbate matters, total pandemonium is introduced when the issue of the dual nature of

130

biblical revelation is introduced, i.e. Scripture is at once a divine and human product. For many, this dual authorship of the text of Scripture would seem to imply that a given passage could have more than one meaning or alternatively, a meaning known only to God and distinct from that known by the author of the text. According to this evangelically popular way of handling predictive passages in the OT, the human author could have a meaning which was restricted to the events proximate to his own day while God, the divine author of the text, could transcend those values with meanings which went far beyond or even dramatically differed from that of the human authors.

Isaiah 7:14 becomes a *crux interpretum* in this exceedingly important, but difficult, debate. Briefly stated, the issue is this: what meaning did Isaiah and God intend for Ahaz when they gave the declaration of Isaiah 7:14 and how does that meaning relate, if at all, to the meaning Matthew derived from that same text, presumably God's fuller meaning, when he pointed it towards the Messiah in Matthew 1:23?

The Hermeneutical case of Protestant orthodoxy, as I understood it is this:

> God's meaning and revelatory-intention in any passageof Scripture may be accurately and confidently ascertained only by studying the verbal meanings of the divinely delegated and inspired human writers. . . That single, original verbal meaning of the human author may be ascertained by heeding the usual literary conventions of history, culture, grammar, syntax, and accumulated theological context.[4]

> No definition of interpretation could be more fundamental than this: *To interpret we must in every case reproduce the sense the Scriptural writer intended for his own words.* The first step in the interpretive process is to link only those ideas with the author's language that he connected with them.[5]

131

Very few evangelicals object to these definitions: divine meanings can be expressed in human words. But that agreement quickly dissolves when this question is asked: "Could God see or intend a sense in a particular text (which is) *separate and different* from that conceived or intended by *his human* instrument?"[6] The key words here are "separate" and "different," for this certainly would introduce double or multiple meanings.

No one denies that texts may legitimately have consequent extensions into later times, cultures and settings. Normally we refer to these extensions of the single meaning of the text as applications, or implications of the general principle (or the universal term) that comes from the author's single meaning. The point where our differences arise comes when we ask if the extension of that meaning, which we obtain from exercising the normal rules of grammar, must be applied *by a continuous extension and from an application of something which is in the same sense,* or may the implications announced also be *different* and *separate* from the grammatico-historical meanings?[7]

When this "consequent sense" is a *different* and an *additional* meaning, allegedly intended only by God, but expressed in words of the author without the author's awareness of their meaning, then we do have an instance of *sensus plenior.* Raymond Brown[8] modified his earlier definition of *sensus plenior* by affirming:

> Let us apply the term *sensus plenior* to that meaning of his text which by normal rules of exegesis would not have been within his awareness or intention but which by other criteria we can determine as having been intended by God. . . We insist that a vague consciousness of this richer meaning may or may not have been present, and that such vague consciousness has no integral place in the definition of the *sensus plenior* either as necessary or as inadmissible.

Surely Brown places this meaning on a different level and uses separate criteria from those exercised in "the normal rules of exegesis.'' What could these separate criteria be? They turn out to be threefold: 1) the development of God's further revelation, 2) the N.T. use of the O.T. tests, and for Catholic exegesis 3) the tradition and *magisterium* of the Church and the church fathers' use of Scripture. The only caveat introduced in the application of these three criteria is this: the fuller sense must not distort or contradict the obvious literal sense of the text; there must be a general resemblance between the fuller and the obvious literal sense which can be checked by comparing this fuller sense with the general direction of Scripture as spelled out in its literal sense.

Now we have very little debate with those who like Professor Donald A. Hagner would go just this far:

> To be aware of sensus plenior is to realize that there is the possibility of more *significance* to an Old Testament passage than was consciously apparent to the original author. . .[9]

But when Hagner continues:

> . . .and more than can be gained by strict grammatic or historical exegesis,''

we must demur. The mistake here becomes clearly stated when Vern Poythress argues on the analogy of the same words being used by two different speakers in separate speeches. He correctly concluded that the same words said by two human authors may yield two separate interpretations.[10] But he appears to stumble when he applies this analogy to Scripture and presses his argument into the mystery of the tri-unity of the Godhead. What the Son says, the Father also says by speaking through him as does the Holy Spirit, explains Poythress. He then applies this truth to the divine/human paradigm of Scripture:

> In Christ's being, there is no pure mathematical identity of divine persons or identity of two natures, but harmony. (This we agree with). The result is that there is no pure mathematical identiy

in the interpretative product. That is, we cannot in a pure way analyze simply what the words mean as (for instance) proceeding from the human nature of Christ, and then say that precisely that, no more, no less, is the exhaustive interpretation of his words.[11]

What must we believe, then, about the success of divine revelation in Scripture? Are we not reduced on this view to adopting either: a) a mechanical view of inspiration in which the author is unwittingly used by God to say and record things which surpass any ligitimate views of human instrumentality, or b) a new view of biblical authority which consistently attributes divine authorization for what can be garnered from the *whole* of Scripture, while the *parts* may only represent the viewpoint of the human author or, at least, a subspecies of divine authority?

Such a differentiation between the levels of authority has already appeared in the evangelical essay by Raju D. Kunjummen. Using the ideal of "intrinsic genre" found in E. D. Hirsch,[12] ("that sense of the whole by means of which an interpreter can correctly understand any part of its determinacy"), Kunjummen also appears to argue for more on the basis of this concept than he should. Indeed, we ourselves have also affirmed, "No meaning of a text is complete until the interpreter has heard the **total single** intention of the author."[13]

But we cannot agree with Kunjummen, who is even bolder than Poythress. Said he:

> The idea of confluence in authorial intention is not a biblical one, though it may be a Thomistic one. Coppens has stated that some object of *sensus plenior* because it 'is contrary to the Thomistic notion of the inspiration whereby Scripture and all its meanings are the result of the joint operation of God and His instrument. . .' This it seems that some evangelicals (apparently this writer) begin with a construct of scholastic philosophy and then

134

attempt to accomodate the phenomena of biblical revelation to it.[14]

This search for normativeness and authority which in some way is at least partially free and autonomous from the human author author who stood in the council of God and originally received that revelation from God is illustrated in the Jesuit Scholar Norbert Lohfink. As we have recorded elsewhere,[15] Lohfink rested his case for biblical authority on what the bible *as a whole* taught. (Previously he had restricted it to what the final redactor of the text taught.[16] Thus for him, in addition to the original sense of the biblical statement there was something above, behind, and beyond what the individual contexts of the bible had to say.

But what could the whole or unity of Scripture teach which could not be found in its parts and individual authors? Lohfink, trapped by his own logic, fled to a "fuller sense" intended by God; yes, a *sensus plenior*. However, Bruce Vawter brilliantly slammed the door shut on *sensus plenior:*

> . . .If this fuller or deeper meaning was reserved by God to Himself and did not enter the writer's purview at all, do we not postulate a Biblical word effected outside the control of the human author's will and judgment. . .and therefore not produced through a truly *human* instrumentality? . . . does not the acceptance of a *sensus plenior* deprive this alleged scriptural sense of one of its essential elements, (and) to that extent . . . it cannot be called scriptural at all?[17]

Kunjummen opposes Vawter's contention that "whatever has been produced apart from the will and judgment . . of the human

author . . has not been brought about precisely through human instrumentality."[18] Instead Kunjummen found that "Scriptural evidence seems to militate against an emphasis which inseparably links human will and judgment to prophetic instrumentality or the human authorship of Scripture."[19] II Peter 1:21, in his view, spoke

135

against the active function of the writer's will in the production of the Scripture. Kunjummen focussed on the prophet's *pheromenoi*, "being borne along" by the Holy Spirit, and therefore he stressed the passivity of the writer's involvement. .

This makes Peter's point somewhat lopsided. He had said in II Peter 1:19-21:

> We have also a more sure word of prophecy; whereunto you do well that you take heed, as to a light shining in a dark place, until the day dawn, and the day star arise in hearts: Knowing this first, that no prophecy of Scripture is (a matter) of one's own loosing (my translation of *epiluseos*). For prophecy came not in old time by the will of man: but Holy men of God spoke as they were moved (borne along) by the Holy Spirit.

Peter's point is not that the prophets were passive or that their "more sure word of prophecy" was a case of their speaking better than they knew. As we have already argued elsewhere: Had Peter's logic been, "Give heed to the light shining in a dark place because no prophet understood or could even explain what he had said (i.e. making *epiluseos* mean "explanation" or "interpretation" since that meaning does occur in Mark 4:34) but he wrote as he was carried along by the Holy Spirit, then that "light" would have been darkness. How could any, including the prophet, then, have given heed to such an enigmatic word?. . Had that communicating ability (of the prophets) not been the case, we would have been forced to ask for a second miracle – the inspiration of the interpreter.[20]

The substantive *epilusis* in its classical usage means a "freeing, loosing" and only secondarily did it come to mean "to explain, unfold, interpret," as in Mark 4:34. Even if this secondary meaning were intended by Peter here, would not even the advocates who claim that the prophets were passive or that they at times "wrote better than they knew" hesitate to say this about all prophetic writings? However, that appears to be the scope of this

136

Petrine word, for the Church is called upon to give heed to this "more sure word of prophecy" as a "light shining in a dark place.' The "light" offered to the modern readers of the prophecies that came in "old time" was possible because God had spoken by these "holy men of God."

What Peter denies is that the product of Scripture may be attributed solely "to the will of man." The initiative, the source, and content of what was revealed to the prophets belonged distinctively to God. But to then argue with Kunjummen that "Human instrumentality in delivering the word of God is frequently depicted in such a way that it does not *demand the full participation* of the speaker's will and judgement"[21] clearly exceeds the biblical data.

In fact, that nexus of the divine source and the human instrument is so close that Paul describes it in I Corinthians 2:6-16 as a sharing of "the deep things of God," which "things were freely given to (the apostles and prophets) by God." These "deep things of God" were so intimately united with the human authors that there was a *veritable living assimilation* of the truth 'taught' by the Holy Spirit (vs 13). Since Paul chose to use the word "taught" (*didaktos*), all mechanical or totally passive ideas of revelation are certainly excluded. Moreover, by "combining spiritual things with spiritual," the apostle teaches us that his Spirit-revealed truths were also clothed in Spirit-taught language, thereby combining what was spiritual in substance with what was spiritual in verbal form.[22]

We conclude, therefore, that it is improper to erect a dual meaning or a multi-tiered level of "readings" to a prophetic text like Isaiah 7:14. We are, however, willing to grant that in addition to what is "in" a text, many texts will sustain "relations" [23] to earlier and, yes, even to later texts. However, recognition of the fact that the *subject* to which a text contributes is almost always larger than any particular contribution to that subject is not tantamount to saying that "things *partially* equal to the same thing are equal to each other." This would be to turn exegesis into the systematic theology: a confusion all too frequently evident in many evangelical methodologies.

II. Isaiah 7:14 and the Single-Meaning Hermeneutic

It is impossible to raise each of the numerous questions that this text has occasioned. Our purpose is much more restricted; we propose to focus on the problem of Isaiah's awareness of the meaning of this text and the legitimacy of relating it simultaneously to Ahaz's day and to the first advent of Messiah. Succinctly stated, our problem is this: if Isaiah intended to predict the advent of Messiah (and this must first be demonstrated that he did), how can this event which occurred seven centuries later be depicted in Isaiah 7 as proximately and inseparably linked with a definite historical event in the immediate future of these eighth century recipients?

What, then, is the central issue which will help us to keep perspective in the midst of the welter of baffling questions? We believe that it is the assurance Isaiah gives in this passage of the permanence of "the house of David" (Isa 7:2).

In fact, the six chapters of Isaiah 7-12 might be entitled, "The Discourse of the three Children" with the pivotal verses coming in Isaiah 8:17-18:

> I will wait for Yahweh,
> Who is hiding his face from the house of Jacob.
> I will put my trust in Him.
> Behold I and the children
> whom Yahweh has given me
> are *signs* and *symbols* in Israel
> from with Yahweh of hosts
> The One dwelling in Mount Zion.[24]

Each of these three children are "signs and each child is born in fulfillment of the promise made to David that his seed should be eternal and that he would have an eternal dominion wielding a peaceful scepter. The three children are:

1. Shear-Jashub = "Remnant-will-return" (7:3) (Compare Isa 10-20, 21, 22; 11:11, 16)

138

2. Immanuel = God-with-us'' (7:14) (Compare Isa 8:8, 10)

3. Maher-Shalal-Hash-Baz = "Hasten-spoil-Hurry-prey'' (8:1, 3, 4) (Compare Isa 10:2, 6)

Consequently, each of the three children is the subject of one introductory prophecy and each is featured later in the argument. In this fact, and in the statement that each of the three children are "signs,'' the children are on the same footing.

But the second child, Immanuel, emerges with a distinctive bearing, separate from the other two children. For one thing, the phraseology used in Isaiah 7:14 would have been reminiscent to Isaiah himself, as well as to his listeners in the eighth century, of previous theophanic appearances of Yahweh. Note these similarities found in the births of Ishmael, Samson, and Isaac:

(a) Isaiah 7:14	"Behold (you) the virgin are pregnant,
(b) Genesis 16:11	"Behold thou are pregnant,
(c) Judges 13:5,7	"Behold thou are pregnant,
(d) Genesis 17:19	"But Sarah your wife

(a^1) and bearing a son,	and shall call his name **Immanuel.**
(b^1) and bearing a son,	and shall call his name **Ishmael.**
(c^1) and bearing a son.	(= **Samson.**)
(d^1) is bearing to thee a son, and you shall call his name **Isaac.**	

No doubt Isaiah's words were deliberately cast in this familiar phraseology so that the prophet's original hearers would associate this new "sign'' of God with those earlier and well-known promises to his people.[25]

But even more impressive is the mention of Immanuel twice in the fourth[26] of these introductory prophecies: Isaiah 8:5-10. Even though the prophesies the fact that the Assyrians will be successful (as exhibited in the fact that Ahaz found more delight in the gods of to which he sacrificed to in Damascus [Isa 8:6; II Chron 28:23; II Kgs 16:10-16] when he later on went to meet their Assyrian conqueror, Tiglath-Pileser) that land – Immanuel's land – will

139

survive. The reason it will survive is simply stated: because of Immanuel himself – "God is with us" (Isa 8:10). Therefore, "Do your worst, you nations . . . Devise your strategy . . . Propose your plan, but it will not stand, because (I am) Immanuel." (Isa 8:9-10; NIV and NIV footnote)!

The truth that God was with them was detailed further in Isaiah 9:1-6 and in Isaiah 11. A child would be born who would sit on the throne of David; a shoot from the stem of Jesse! As Willis J. Beecher concluded:

> It may be doubted whether any of them had in mind the idea of just such a person as Jesus, to be born of a virgin, in some future century; but they had in mind some birth in the unending line of David which would render the truth "God with us," especially significant.[27]

Our argument is that this passage cannot be fairly handled until it is seen as another prediction in the series of promises made with "the house of David." Once this proposition is grasped, it is possible to proceed to the more difficult question: how is the promise made with the house of David to be linked with a "sign" which functions for Ahaz's generation and that final "shoot" that will come from the "stump of Jesse," whose name will be "Wonderful Counselor, Mighty God, Everlasting Father, Prince of Peace?" This is the question that has made interpreters return to this text time and time again.

The historical setting is well know by now to all interpreters, even if it can only be sketched in general terms. Rezin, the reigning monarach in Damascus, Syria and Pekah, the ruler of the Israelite throne in Samaria, plotted together to teach the house of David and its present holder of the throne, Ahaz, a lesson. They proposed to set "The son of Tabeel" (Isa 7:6) on the throne in Jerusalem in place of a scion of David.

Even before Ahaz became King, Rezin and Pekah had already begun to encroach on Judean territory during the reign of Ahaz's predecessor, Jothan, (II Kgs 15:37). Clearly these two northern nemeses wanted Jothan, and then Ahaz, to join their anti-Assyrian coalition, but these Davidites and the population of Jerusalem wanted no part in stirring up the wrath of Nineveh. Miller and Hayes[28] suggest that the cities denounced by the prophet Micah in his first chapter may indeed have been towns in the prophet's neighborhood who were anti-Assyrian and therefore opposed Ahaz's pro-Assyrian policy.

It is extremely important to note, therefore, that the attack on Jerusalem in Ahaz's reign was the climax to a war that had originally broken out in Jothan's reign and the intervention of the Assyrians was not the cause of it, nor its beginning.

In place of the current Davidic ruler, Pekah and Rezin intended to place "the son of Tabeel." What were the motives that impelled Pekah and Rezin to challenge Jotham and Ahaz? Was the key to be sought in the military struggle for Transjordania as B. Obed[29] suggests is the case on the basis of II Chronicles 27:5 where Jotham defeated the Ammonites and exacted a heavy tribute from them? Obed believes that this "ben-Tobeel" can be traced back through Tobiah the Ammonite servant (Neh 2:19; 6:17; Zech 6:10) to a grandson of the Tobiah known from the Lachish letters, up to Ben Tobeel in the time of Ahaz.[30]

Others make the unnamed son of Tabeel a son or relative of King Tubail = Tabeel, the ruling house in Tyre who were strong supporters of the anti-Assyrian coalition.[31] It is impossible to say who he was or from whence he came.

For our purposes, the challenge to the Davidic dynasty, and thereby to the program of redemptive history, is the only point which emerges clearly in this complicated issue. Isaiah assured a worried Ahaz that the two Northern partners opposing him with all their threats would be doomed to failure.

Whether the movements of the Assyrian King Tiglath-pileser were motivated by Ahaz's request for help in II KIngs 16:7, or by strategies that may even have preceeded that, is an open question.

141

What is known is that Tiglath-pileser did undertake a campaign against Syria-Palestine in 738 B.C. In the Annuls of Tiglath-pileser III, paragraph 772,[32] we are told of the number of captives he took from each city along with the fact that he received tribute from a Menihumnu (=Menahem) of Samaria and Hahianu (= Rezin) of Aram (Damascus). Four years later in 734 B.C., again according to the Assyrian annals, Tiglath-pileser invaded Philistia.[33]

What, then, is the chronological relation between the Syro-Ephraimite War and the 738 and 734 campaiagn of Tiglath-pileser? We know that 732 ended the allies adventure, but as Michael Thompson asks, "How is it possible to conceive of Rezin and Pekah essaying an anti-Assyrian movement when the Assyrian army was already in Syria-Palestine?"[34]

Thompson is forced to conclude, as we are, that "The war must have occurred, there, *before* Tiglath-pileser's 734 campaign against Philistia, and it is credible that its associated anti-Assyrian mood should have been strengthened and encouraged in the years following the earlier Assyrian campaign in 738."[35]

Herbert Donner [36] objects to this reconstruction arguing that there is not enough time between Pekah's accession to the throne in 735 B.C. and Tiglath-pileser's intervention in 734. But Pekah's reign is shrouded in such darkness that none can set any firm date for his accession to the throne. In Edwin Theile's[37] construction, he began his reign in 752 B.C. and reigned, perhaps at first in the Transjordanean territory just south of Damascus, and then in Samaria for a total of twenty years until his death in 732 B.C.

The advantage of placing the beginnings of the Syro-Ephraimitish War **before** the Assyrian campaign of 734 B.C. is clear: ". . .we can perhaps more easily understand why Rezin and Pekah might have thought that their anti-Assyrian plans had some hope of succeeding. For they enjoyed a period of years – perhaps three, or even longer – when they had been free of the Assyrian and had thus had time (due to Tiglath-pileser's occupation with matters in the north and the south of his empire so that the west was spared any incursions)."[38]

All of this only peaks our curiosity all the more: what was the year that Isaiah delivered his message to Ahaz? It had to be prior to 734 B.C. How much more we cannot say.

But the door is now opened for a new look at the old question: What child born in Ahaz's day served as a sign to his generation while also embodying the wonderful names of that coming Davidic prince? We believe the best working hypothesis still is the one that says that Ahaz's son Hezekiah is the best candidate.[39]

However, that suggestion raises the most nettlesome problem of all. To say that the chronology of this period is obscure is to understate the magnitude of the difficulty. The principle areas of difficulty come in harmonizing the chronological data of II Kings 15-18. The issues may be listed as follows:

1. If Hezekiah was 25 years old at his accession according to II Kings 18:2, and if his accession is placed in 714 B.C. (the latest date anyone proposes), he must have been born in 739 B.C.

2. If Hezekiah's father was 20 at his own accession to the throne and he reigned for 16 years (II Kgs 16:1-2), he would have died when he was 36 (when Hezekiah apparently was 25), making Ahaz only 11 when his son Hezekiah was born!

3. To exacerbate matters still further, the chronological data of II Kings 18:1, 9, 10 make the fifth year of Hezekiah's reign the same year that Samaria fell in 722 (II Kgs 18:10); therefore Hezekiah succeeded his father Ahaz in 726-27 B.C., meaning Hezekiah would have been born twenty-five years earlier in 752-51! Very few opt for the 752 B.C. date, for most equate Hezekiah's fourteenth year of his reign with Sennacherib's invasion in 701 B.C.[40]

The year 701 B.C. appears to be the pivotal year. For the moment let us not decide whether that is Hezekiah's fourteenth or twenty-fourth reigning year. Instead, let us skip down in the list two rulers to King Josiah who met his death at 39 years of age in 609 B.C.

143

after ruling for 31 years (II Kgs 22:1). This 609 B.C. date is secure because the events associated with Josiah's death are recorded in Babylonian Chronicle on a year by year basis.[41]

Josiah was preceeded by Amon, who reigned for two years (II Kgs 21:19) and he in turn was preceeded by Manasseh who ruled for 55 years (II Kgs 21:1). Now 609 plus 31 = 640, plus 2 = 642, plus 55 = 697 B.C.

But there must be a coregency between Manasseh and Hezekiah since Hezekiah's 29 years (II Kgs 18:2) would last until 686 B.C. if his fourteenth year matches Sennacherib's invasion of 701 B.C. Moreover, II Kings 20:1 states: "In those days Hezekiah became ill and was at the point of death" when Isaiah told him "Put your house in order, because you will die; you will not recover." What would be more natural than for him to place his son on the throne as a coregent at such a desperate point in his life?

No doubt when Manasseh had reached the age of twelve (the accepted year of maturity in the Jewish community, cf. Lk. 2:42, 49), he made him a coregent. And in response to Hezekiah's prayer, God extended his life fifteen years - eleven of which he ruled with his son as coregent from 697-686 B.C.

This solution does not help us with the synchronisms given with Hoshea in II Kings 18:1, 9, 10. In fact, Edwin Thiele,[42] that great solver of every other synchronism and chronological fact in the chronologies of the Hebrew Kings simply gave up when he came to this one in his doctoral study submitted to the University of Chicago. Thiele argued that the reign of Hoshea was over and the Kingdom of Israel no longer existed when Hezekiah came to the throne. His evidence is this: one of Hezekiah's first acts was to repair the temple in the first month of his first year (II Chron 29:3, 17) and then to proclaim the celebration of the Passover on the fourteenth day of the second month (II Chron 30:2, 13, 15). His invitations, however, were not limited to Judah, but he sent to "all Israel and Judah" including Ephraim, Manasseh, Zebulun, and Asher (II Chron 30:1, 6, 10, 11), areas once securely in the hands of the Northern Kingdom who had issued strict warnings against

144

going to Jerusalem to celebrate anything. Indeed, he sent his decree "throughout all Israel, from Beersheba even to Dan" (II Chron 30:5-). Clearly, argues Thiele, Samaria had fallen.

Now if some emend II Kings 18:13 and Isaiah 36:1 to read "twenty-four" instead of "fourteen," John McHugh suggests that we emend II Kings 18:2 instead. He proposes that Hezekiah was only "fifteen" years old, not "twenty-five" when he came to the throne, therefore Hezekiah would have been born in 731/730 B.C.43 and thus his birth would have coincided with Judah's deliverance from the Syro-Ephraimite alliance.

However, there is no more textual evidence for this emendation than there was for the one suggsted for II Kings 18:13 and Isaiah 36:1. In our view, the events that precipitated Isaiah's warnings may have come as early as 740 or 739 B.C., just prior to Tiglath-pileser's 738 foray into this territory. One fact remains: this scrap did not begin with Ahaz; it had roots in the last days of Ahaz's predecessor, King Jotham.

When the data is further massaged and refined by some new discoveries we believe it will locate Hezekiah's birth and Isaiah's rebuke to Ahaz at some date early in this decade, perhaps four to six years prior to the fall of Damascus and the deaths of Pekah and Rezin in 732 B.C.

How would such an identity relate to Messiah who came seven centuries later? The same way that many of the "generic prophecies" of the OT link the immediate fulfillment with the distant fulfillment. Willis J. Beecher defined a "generic prediction/promise" this way:

> A generic prediction is one which regards an event as occurring in a series of parts, separated by intervals, and expresses itself in language that may apply indifferently to the nearest part, or to the remoter parts, or the the whole – in other words, a prediction which, in applying to the whole of a complex event, also applies to some of its parts."[44]

This is not to argue for a double sense or multiple meaning; instead, this definition seeks to represent the biblical facts which demand that the near and the distant were, in some real sense, linked in the prophetic revelatory vision from God. Accordingly, Antiochus Epiphanes is the Antichrist in Daniel 11 even though that same chapter, along with I John 2:18, looked forward to a final future Antichrist even if "Many antichrists have (already) come" (I Jh 2:18b). Likewise, Elijah the prophet must come before that great and dreadful day of the Lord (Mal 4:5) even if John the Baptist was Elijah (since he came in the spirit and the power" of Elijah – Lk 1:17). Both aspects of this identity were in Jesus' own words: "(John the Baptist) is Elijah (Matt 11:14) and "Elijah is coming and he will restore all things" (Matt 17:11).

If some protest, "yes but,Hezekiah was not born of a virgin!", we will point out that neither Antiochus Epiphanes nor John the Baptist mirrored every or even most of the details which their final fulfiller will demonstrate. The only critical point is that both share enough distinctive common elements so that a single sense and meaning links them and thereby the one heeding Scripture will be unerringly pointed towards the final fulfillment. In this case, the most essential common feature shared is that both Hezekiah and Messiah were from "the House of David which God had promised would never perish."

Walter C. Kaiser, Jr.
Academic Dean
Professor of Old Testament and Semitic Languages
Trinity Evangelical Divinity School
Deerfield, Illinios, 60015
USA

[1]J. Skinner. *The Book of the Prophet Isaiah*, Chapters 1 - XXXIX. Cambridge Bible, Cambridge: Cambridge University, 1905, p. 60.

[2]Brevard S. Childs, *Isaiah and the Assyrian Crisis*. London: SCM, 1967, p. 120.

[3]H. H. Rowley, "Hezekiaah's Reform and Rebellion," in *Men of God: Studies in Old Testament History and Prophecy*. London: Thomas Nelson & Sons, Ltd., 1963, pp 111-12.

[4]Walter C. Kaiser, Jr. "The Single Intent of Scripture," in *Evangelical Roots: A Tribute to Wilbur Smith*, ed. Kenneth S. Kantzer. Nashville: Nelson, 1978, p. 138.

[5]Walter C. Kaiser, Jr. "Legitimate Hermeneutics," in *Inerrancy,* ed. Norman L. Geisler. Grand Rapids: Zondervan, 1977, p. 118.

[6]Walter C. Kaiser, Jr. "A Response to 'Author's Intention and Biblical Interpretation,'" in *Hermeneutics, Inerrancy, and the Bible,* ed. Earl D. Radmacher and Robert D. Preus. Grand Rapids: Zondervan, 1984, p. 442 (italics my own).

[7]See our essay "A Response to 'Author's Intention and Biblical Interpretation,'" *ibid.,* pp 441-447. Note also the seminal articles on this topic by C. F. DeVine, "The Consequent Sense," *Catholic Biblical Quarterly* 2(1940): 145-55 and Rudolph Bierberg, "Does Sacred Scripture Have A Sensus Plenior?" *Catholic Biblical Quaraterly* 10(1948): 182-95.

[8]Raymond E. Brown, "The Sensus Plenior in the Last Ten Years," Catholic Biblical Quarterly 25(1963): 268-69.

[9]Donald A. Hagner, "The Old Testament in the New Testament," in *Interpreting the Word of God,* ed. Samauel Schultz and Morris Inch, Chicago: Moody Press, 1976, p. 72 (Italics ours.)

[10]Vern S. Poythress, "Divine Meaning of Scripture," *Westminster Theological Journal* 48(1986): 255.

[11]Vern S. Poythress, *ibid,* p 263.

[12]E. D. Hirsch *Validity in Interpretation.* New Haven: Yale, 1967, pp 61-2.

[13]Walter C. Kaiser, Jr. "Legitimate Hermenuetics," p. 127.

[14]Raju D. Kunjummen, "The Single Intent of Scripture – Critical Examination of a Theological Construct," *Grace Theological Journal* 7(1986): 100. The citation of Joseph Coppens is found in his essay, "The Different Senses of Sacred Scripture," *Theological Digest* 1 (1953): 18.

[15]Walter C. Kaiser, Jr. *Towards an Exegetical Theology.* Grand Rapids: Baker, 1981, pp 109-110.

[16]Norbert Lohfink. *The Christian Meaning of the Old Testament.* tr. R. A. Wilson, Milwaukee: Bruce, 1968, pp 32-49.

[17]Bruce Vawter. *Biblical Inspiration.* Theological Resources. Philadelphia: Westminster, 1972, p. 115. Also see Walter C. Kaiser, Jr. "The Fallacy of Equating Meaning with the Reader's Understanding," *Trinity Journal* 6 (1977): 190-93.

[18]Bruce Vawter, "The Fuller Sense: Some Considerations," *Catholic Biblical Quarterly* 26(1964): 93.

[19]Raju D. Kunjummen, "The Single Intent," p. 99.

[20]Walter C. Kaiser, Jr. *The Uses of the Old Testament in the New.* Chicago: Moody, 1985, pp 75-6.

[21]Raju Kunjummen, "The Single Intent," p. 99 (italics ours)

[22]See our extended discussion of this extremely important teaching passage on this doctrine: Walter C. Kaiser, Jr. "A Neglected Text in Bibliology Discussions: I Corintiahsn 2:6-16," *Westminster Theological Journal* 43(1981): 301-19; especially pp 315-18.

[23]A point accurately made by Vern Poythress, "Divine Meaning," pp 273-76. Beautifully he declares, "Hence, scholars are correct in taking care to distinguish what comes from the psalm itself and what comes from the psalm seen in the light of the whole Bible." I would just delete the second "comes from the psalm." But Vern goes no to spoil this division of labor by affirming, "God does say more, now, through (Psalm 22) than he said to the OT readers. The 'more' arises from the stage of fuller revelation, and consequent fuller

illumination of the Holy Spirit, in which we live.'' (p. 275). Apparently we believers have a revelation of interpretation parallel to the revelation of the words which the authors received.

[24]Translation and italics my own.

[25]This point and the whole organization of the argument about the three children has been taken from Willis J. Beecher, "The Prophecy of the Virgin Mother: Isa vvi. 14,'' in *Homiletical Review* 17(1889): 354-58. This essay was reprinted in *Classical Evangelical Essays in Old Testament Interpretation*. ed. Walter C. Kaiser, Jr. Grand Rapids: Baker, 1972, pp 179-85. Note also the clear eight scene outline of Louis Brodie, "The Children and the Prince: The Structure, Nature and Date of Isaiah 6-12,'' *Biblical Theology Bulletin*, 9(1979): 27-31. Said he, "And just as there is a continuity between the children of Isaiah (in scenes 1, 3, 5 and 7) so we expect a continuity between Immanuel (Scenes 2 and 4) and the Davidic prince (Scenes 6 and 8),'' p 29.

[26]The other three are: Isaiah 7:2-9; 7:10-25; 8:1-4.

[27]Willis J. Beecher, "The Prophecy of the Virgin Mother,'' p 358.

[28]J. Maxwell Miller and John H. Hayes. *A History of Ancient Israel and Judah.* Philadelphia: Westminster, 1986, p 344. This anti-Assyrian thesis was first proposed by J. Begrich, "Der Syrisch-Ephraimitische Krieg und seine weltpolitischen zusammenhange,'' *Zeitschrift der Deutsch morgenlandischen Gesellschaft* 83(1929): 213-37.

[29]B. Obed, "The Historical Background of the Syro-Ephraimite War Reconsidered,'' *Catholic Biblical Quarterly* 34(1972): 155. For a critique of Obed's views see Michael E. W. Thompson. *Situation and Theology: Old Testament Interpretations of the Syro-Ephraimite War.* Sheffield, Almond, 1982, pp 107-109.

[30]B.Obed, "The Historical Background,'' p 161. He cites B. Mazar, "The Tobiads,'' *Israel Exploration Journal* 7(1957): 233-34; 236-37.

[31]Miller and Hayes, *A History of Ancient Israel,* p 342.

[32]D.D. Luckenbill. *Ancient Records of Assyria and Babylonia.* New York: Greenwood, 1968, 1: 276.

[33]More detailed information about the campaign is contained in the inscription ND 400 which was discovered in 1950 in the excavations in Nimrud. See Donald J. Wiseman, "Two Historical Inscriptions from Nimrud,'' Iraq 13(1951): 21-26.

[34]Michael Thompson. *Situation and Theology,* p 111.

[35]Michael Thompson. *Situation and Theology,* p 111. Two other scholars may be cited as agreeing with locating the war prior to 734: John Bright. A History of Israel 2nd ed. Phila.: Westminster Press, 1972, p 272; Norman K. Gottwald. *All the Kingdoms of the Earth: Israelite Prophecy and International Relations in the Ancient Near East.* New York: Harper and Row, 1964, p 149.

[36]Herbert Donner. "The Separate States of Israel and Judah,'' in *Israelite and Judean History,* eds. John H. Hayes and J. Maxwell Miller, London: SCM, 1977, p 429.

[37]Edwin R. Thiele. *A Chronology of the Hebrew Kings.* Grand Rapids: Zondervan, 1977, pp 52-3.

[38]Michael Thompson. *Situation and Theology,* pp 111-12.

[39]This suggestion was previously favored by Jewish interpreters and is currently advocated by scholars such as John Lindblom. *A Study on the Immanuel Section in Isaiah:* Isa

vii, 1-ix, 6. London: C.W.K. Gleerup, 1958, p. 25; John McHugh, "The Date of Hezekiah's Birth," *Vetus Testamentum*. 14(1964): 446-53; E. Hammershaimb, "The Immanuel Sign," *Studia Theologia cura ordinum theologorum Scandinavicorum edita, III* (1949): p 135.

[40]It is true that H. H. Rowley, "Hezekiah's Reform and Rebellion," In Men of God, p 113 proposes to correct the Hebrew text *'arba' 'eseh* ("four and ten" - "fourteen") to *'arba' w''es'rim* ("four and twenty" = "twenty-four"). Likewise Gleason Archer, *Encyclopia of Bible Difficulties*. Grand Rapids: Zondervan, 1982, p 211, says "We must therefore conclude that the Masoretic text has preserved an ancient textual error (which also appears in Isa 36:1 – where the error probably originated), in which a mistake was made in the decade column. The word 'fourteen' was originally 'twenty-four'."

[41]Donald J. Wiseman. *The Chronicles of the Chaldaean Kings(626-556 B.C.) in the British Museum*. London: British Museum, 1956, p 63.

[42]Edwin Thiele, *A Chronology,* pp 53-4.

[43]John McHugh, "The Date of Hezekiah's Birth," p 452.

[44]Willis J. Beecher. *The Prophets and the Promise*. Grand Rapids: Baker, 1963 (1905 r.p.), p 130.

Bibliography for References Cited

Throughout this book the numbers in parentheses refer to footnotes and mean the following: the first number refers to the book in the bibliography with that number. The numbers after the colon refer to the page numbers in the book cited. Where a book has two volumes, we have identified the volume with Roman numeral I or II.

(Starred texts are recommended reading.)

1. Walter C. Kaiser, Jr., *The Old Testament in Contemporary Preaching*, Grand Rapids, MI, Baker, 1973.

*2. Walter C. Kaiser, Jr., *The Uses of the Old Testament in the New*, Chicago, Moody Press, 1985.

*3. Willis Judson Beecher, *The Prophets and the Promise*, Grand Rapids, MI, Baker, 1970 (rpt. 1905).

4. Norman Geisler, *A Popular Survey of the Old Testament*, Grand Rapids, MI, Baker, 1978.

5. Arthur W. Kac, *The Messiahship of Jesus: What Jews and Jewish Christians Say*, Chicago, Moody Press, 1980.

*6. Charles Lee Feinberg, *Is the Virgin Birth in the Old Testament?*, Whittier, CA, Emeth Publications, 1967.

*7. Norman Geisler, *Christ: The Theme of the Bible*, Chicago, Moody Press, 1969.

8. Gershom Scholam, *The Messianic Idea in Judaism and Other Essays on Jewish Spirituality*, New York, Schocken Books, 1971.

9. Sir Robert Anderson, *The Coming Prince: The Marvelous Prophecy of Daniel's Seventy Weeks Concerning the Antichrist*, Grand Rapids, MI, Kregel, 1977.

10. Pinchas Lapide and Ulrich Luz, *Jesus in Two Perspectives: a Jewish-Christian Dialogue*, Minneapolis, MN, Ogsburg, 1985.

11. A. Cohen, *Everyman's Talmud*, New York, Schocken Books, 1978.

12. Good News Society, *How to Recognize the Messiah*, Johannesburg, MD.

13. Moishe Rosen, *Y'shua: The Jewish Way to Say Jesus*, Chicago, Moody Press, 1982.

14. Raphael Patai, *The Messiah Texts*, New York, Avon, 1979.

15. James A. Borland, *Christ in the Old Testament: A Comprehensive Study of Old Testament Appearances of Christ in Human Form*, Chicago, Moody, 1979.

16. Fred John Meldau, *Messiah in Both Testaments*, Denver, CO, Christian Victory, 1967.

17. Harold W. Hoehner, *Chronological Aspects of the Life of Christ*, Grand Rapids, MI, Zondervan/Academie, 1977.

18. Marc H. Tanenbaum, et. al. (eds.), *Evangelicals and Jews in Conversation on Scripture, Theology, and History*, Grand Rapids, MI, Baker Book House, 1978.

19. Peter W. Stoner, *Science Speaks: Scientific Proof of the Accuracy of Prophecy and the Bible*, Chicago, Moody Press, 1969.

20. Arthur W. Kac, *The Messianic Hope: A Divine Solution for the Human Problem*, Grand Rapids, MI, Baker, 1975.

21. Fred John Maldau, *Christ the Prophet*, Denver, CO, Christian Victory, 1968.

22. E. W. Hengstenberg, *Christology of the Old Testament*, MacDill AFB, Florida, MacDonald Publshing, nd.

23. Marc H. Tanenbaum, et. al. (eds), *Evangelicals and Jews in an Age of Pluralism*, Grand Rapids, MI, Baker Book House, 1984.

24. Hugh J. Schonfeld, *The Passover Plot*, New York, Bantam, 1969.

25. Rabbi Yechiel Eckstein, *What Christians Should Know About Jews and Judaism*, Waco, TX, Word, 1984.

26. Mal Couch, *Rabbinical Views of Messianic Passages*, nd. np.

27. The International School of Biblical Research, *The Messiah of the Targums, Talmuds and Rabbinical Writers*, Montrose, CA, International School of Biblical Research, nd.

28. Arnold G. Fruchtenbaum, *The Footsteps of the Messiah: A Study of the Sequence of Prophetic Events*, San Antonio, TX, Ariel Press, 1982.

29. Elwood McQuaid, *The Outpouring: Jesus in the Feasts of Israel*, Chicago, Moody Press, 1986.

*30. Walter C. Kaiser, Jr., *Toward an Old Testament Theology*, Grand Rapids, MI, Zondervan, 1978.

31. John F. Walvoord, *Daniel: the Key to Prophetic Revelation*, Chicago, Moody Press, 1972.

*32. Henry Morris, *Many Infallible Proofs: Practical and Useful Evidences of Christianity*, San Diego, CA, Creation Life Publishers, 1974.

33. Josh McDowell, *Evidence That Demands a Verdict: Historical Evidences for the Christian Faith*, San Bernardino, CA, Campus Crusade for Christ/Here's Life Publishers, rev. 1979.

34. Emile Borel, *Probabilities and Life*, New York, Dover, 1962, chs. 1-3.

*35. Robert Glenn Gromacki, *The Virgin Birth of Christ*, New York, Thomas Nelson, 1974.

36. James Gunn, *Christ: the Fullness of the Godhead*, Neptune, NJ, Loizeaux Brothers, 1983.

37. H. C. Leupold, *Exposition of Isaiah* (one volume edition), Grand Rapids, MI, Baker, 1971.

38. J. Gresham Machen, *The Virgin Birth of Christ*, Grand Rapids, MI, Baker, 1930, 1971.

39. Harry Rimmer, *The Magnificence of Jesus: a Study in Christology*, Grand Rapids, MI, Eerdmans, 1943.

*40. Wilbur M. Smith, *The Supernaturalness of Christ*, Grand Rapids, MI, Baker, 1974 rpt.

41. Merrill Unger, *Unger's Commentary on the Old Testament*, Chicago, Moody, 1981.

42. Edward J. Young, *The Book of Isaiah*, Vol. 1, Grand Rapids, MI, Erdmans, 1976.

43. Leon Wood, *A Commentary on Daniel*, Grand Rapids, MI, Zondervan.

44. A. J. McClain, *Daniel's Prophecy of the Seventy Weeks*, Grand Rapids, MI, Zondervan.

45. Josh McDowell, *Daniel in the Critics' Den*, San Bernardino, CA, Campus Crusade.

46. Joachim Becker, *Messianic Expectation in the Old Testament*, Philadlelphia, Fortress Press, 1980.

*47. Alfred Edersheim, *The Life and Times of Jesus the Messiah* (one volume edition), Grand Rapids, MI, Eerdmans, 1972.

48. David Baron, *Commentary on Zechariah, His Visions and Prophecies*, Grand Rapids, MI, Kregel, 1988 (rpt.)

49. H. L. Ellison, *The Centrality of the Messianic Idea for the Old Testament*, Tyndale, 1953.

50. James Coppedge, *Evolution: Possible or Impossible?*, Grand Rapids, MI, Zondervan, 1973.

*51. Charles Briggs, *Messianic Prophecy*, New York, Schribners, 1889.

*52. Franz Delitzsch and Paton Gloag, *The Messiahship of Christ [the Messianic Prophecies of Christ]*, Minneapolis, MN, Klock & Klock, 1983 rpt. [See book II, pp. 31-38, for additional important literature]. Part One: Franz Delitzsch, *The Messianic Prophecies in Historical Succession* (Lectures delivered at the Institutum Judaicum, 1887); Part Two: Paton J. Gloag, *The Messianic Prophecies* (The Baird Lectures for 1879 at the University of Glasgow).

53. Walter Kaiser, Jr., "Messianic Prophecies in the Old Testament" in Carl Amerding and Ward Gasque (eds.), *Handbook of Biblical Prophecy*, Grand Rapids, MI, Baker, 1980.

54. Gerald Sigal, *The Jew and the Christian Missionary: a Jewish Response to Missionary Christianity*, New York, KTAV Press, 1981.

*55. David Baron, *Rays of Messiah's Glory: Christ in the Old Testament*, Grand Rapids, MI, Zondervan, 1886.

56. Transcript, *Do the Messianic Prophecies of the Old Testament Point to Jesus or Someone Else?* with Drs. Walter Kaiser, Jr. and Pinchas Lapide, Chattanooga, TN, The John Ankerberg Evangelistic Association, 1985.

57. C. F. Keil, F. Delitzsch, *Commentary on the Old Testament in Ten Volumes* (James Martin, trans.) (Vol. VII, Isaiah), Grand Rapids, MI, Eerdmans, 1978.

58. Edward J. Young, *The Book of Isaiah*, Vol. 1, Grand Rapids, MI, Eerdmans, 1972.

59. "The Divine Messiah in the Old Testament," Benjamin B. Warfield, *Biblical and Theological Studies*, Philadelphia, PA, Presbyterian & Reformed, 1968.

60. Edward J. Young, *The Book of Isaiah*, Vol. 3, Grand Rapids, MI, Eerdmans, 1972.

61. Theo. Laetsch, *Bible Commentary: Jeremiah*, St. Louis, MO, Concordia, 1965.

62. Frank Gaebelein (ed.), *The Expositors Bible Commentary* (Vol. 7, Daniel and the Minor Prophets), Grand Rapids, MI, Zondervan, 1985.

63. Homer Hailey, *A Commentary on the Minor Prophets*, Grand Rapids, MI, Baker, 1976.

64. C. F. Keil, F. Delitzsch, *Commentary on the Old Testament, Vol. 10: Minor Prophets*, Grand Rapids, MI, Eerdmans, 1978.

*65. Ceil and Moishe Rosen, *Christ in the Passover*, Chicago, Moody Press, 1980.

66. Victor Buksbazen, *The Gospel in the Feasts of Israel*, Fort Washington, PA, Christian Literature Crusade, 1954.

67. Arthur W. Pink, *The Divine Inspiration of the Bible*, Grand Rapids, MI, Baker, 1971.

*68. William Lane Craig, *The Son Rises: Historical Evidence for the Resurrection of Jesus*, Chicago, Moody, 1981.

69. Gary R. Habermas, *Ancient Evidence for the Life of Jesus: Historical Records of His Death and Resurrection*, New York, Thomas Nelson, 1984.

70. Pinchas Lapide, *The Resurrection of Jesus: A Jewish Perspective*, Minneapolis, MN, Augsburg, 1983.

71. John Bowker, *The Targums and Rabbinic Literature*, London, Cambridge University Press, 1969.

72. Aaron Judah Kligerman, *Messianic Prophecy in the Old Testament*, Grand Rapids, MI, Zondervan, 1957.

73. J. F. Stenning (ed.), *The Targum of Isaiah*, London, Oxford Press, 1949.

74. Jacob Gartenhaus, *Famous Hebrew Christians*, Grand Rapids, MI, Baker, 1979.

*75. Zola Levitt, *Some of My Best Friends Are Christians*, Glendale, CA, Regal, 1978.

76. William Wilson, *Wilson's Old Testament Word Studies*, McLean, VA, MacDonald Publishing Company, n.d.

77. H. C. Leupold, *Exposition of Genesis*, Grand Rapids, MI, Baker, 1978.

78. No. 57, Vol. 1: The Pentateuch.

79. John Bowker, *The Targums and Rabbinic Literature*, London, Cambridge University Press, 1969.

80. J. W. Ethridge, *The Targums of Onkelos and Jonathan Ben Ussiel on the Pentateuch*, Vols. 1, 2, New York, KTAV Publishing, 1968.

81. Ralph A. Martin, "The Earliest Messianic Interpretation of Genesis 3:15," *Journal of Biblical Literature*, Vol. 84 (1965), pp. 425-427.

82. Nahum N. Glatzer, *Hammer on the Rock: A Short Midrash Reader*, New York, Schocken, 1969.

83. Hermann L. Strack, *Introduction to the Talmud and Midrash*, New York, Atheneum/Jewish Publication Society of America, 1969.

84. William G. Braude (trans.), *The Midrash on Psalms*, Vol. 1, New Haven, Hale University Press, 1959.

85. Maurice H. Harris, *Hebraic Literature: Translations from the Talmud Midrashim and Kabbala*, New York, Tudor, 1943.

86. Isidore Singer (ed.), *The Jewish Encyclopedia*, New York, Funk and Wagnalls, 1916.

87. David Berger, Michael Wyschogrod, *Jews and "Jewish Christianity"*, New York, KTAV Publishing, 1978.

88. H. L. Ellison, *The Centrality of the Messianic Idea for the Old Testament*, London, Tyndale, 1953.

89. Walter Kaiser, Jr., "The Promise of Isaiah 7:14 and the Single Meaning Hermeneutic" (The Ritter Lecture for 1987 at Evangelical School of Theology).

90. No. 57, Vol. 5: The Psalms

91. John Peter Lange, *Commentary on the Holy Scriptures Vol. 5, Psalms - Song of Solomon*, Grand Rapids, MI, Zondervan, 1980.

92. J. Gresham Machen, *The Virgin Birth of Christ*, Grand Rapids, MI, Baker, 1971.

93. Hal Lindsey, *The Promise*, Irvine, CA, Harvest House, 1974.

94. Ben Blisheim, "Messianic Judaism - An Alternative," privately published.

95. Francis Brown, S. R. Driver, Charles A. Briggs, *A Hebrew and English Lexicon of the Old Testament*, London, Oxford University Press, 1968.

96. Pierre Barbet, *A Doctor at Calvary: The Passion of Our Lord Jesus Christ as Described by a Surgeon*, Garden City, NY, Doubleday/Image, 1963. (cf. C. Truman David, M.D., "The Crucifixion of Jesus," *New Wine*, August 1971.)

97. W. Gunther Plaut et. al., *The Torah - A Modern Commentary*, New York, Union of American Hebrew Congregations, 1981.

98. Kenneth Barker (gen. ed.), *The NIV Study Bible (New International Version)*, Grand Rapids, MI, Zondervan, 1985, (seventh printing).

*99. American Board of Missions to the Jews, *Introducing the Jewish People to Their Messiah*, Orangeburg, NY, ABMJ, 1977.

*100. Zola Levitt, *Jews and Jesus*, Chicago, Moody, 1977.

*101. Lee Amber, *Chosen: Communicating With Jews of All Faiths*, Santa Ana, CA, Vision House, 1981.

102. The Jewish Publication Society, *Tanakh: A New Translation of the Holy Scriptures According to the Traditional Hebrew Text*, New York, The Jewish Publication Society, 1985.

103. H. C. Leupold, *Exposition of Daniel*, Grand Rapids, MI, Baker, 1981.

104. Gleason L. Archer, Jr. (Tr.), *Jerome's Commentary on Daniel*, Grand Rapids, MI, Baker, 1977.

105. R. S. Driver, Neubauer, *The Jewish Interpreters of Isaiah 53*, New York, KTAV, 1969.

106. E. J. Young, *The Prophecy of Daniel: A Commentary*, Grand Rapids, MI, Eerdmans, 1978.

107. Robert Dick Wilson, *Studies in the Book of Daniel* (One Vol., ed.), Grand Rapids, MI, Baker, 1979.

108. No. 57, Vol. 10: The Minor Prophets.

109. T. V. Moore, *Zechariah, Haggai and Malachi*, Carlisle, PA, Banner of Ti h Trust, 1974.

110. J. D. Douglas, *New Bible Dictionary*, Grand Rapids, MI, Eerdmans, 1970.

111. Judge Clarence Bartlett, *As a Lawyer Sees Jesus*, Cincinnati, OH, Standard Publishing, 1960.

112. Irwin Linton, *A Lawyer Examines the Bil ie: A Defense of the Christian Faith*, San Diego, CA, Creation-Life Publishers, 1977.

113. John Warwick Montgomery, *The Shape of the Past: A Christian Response to Secular Philosophies of History*, Minneapolis, MN, Bethany, 1975.

114. R. C. Sproul, "The Case for Inerrancy: A Methodological Analysis" in John Warwick Montgomery (ed.), *God's Inerrant Word: An International Symposiu.n on the Trustworthiness of Scripture*, Minneapolis, MN, Bethany, 1974.

115. No. 91, Vol. 7: Ezekiel-Malachi.

116. Josh McDowell, *More Evidence That Demands a Verdict: Historical Evidences for the Christian Scriptures* (Rev.), San Bernardino, CA: Here's Life Publishers, 1981.

117. William Whiston (tr.), *The Works of Flavius Josephus*, Grand Rapids, MI, Baker, 1984 (4 Vols.).

118. John Warwick Montgomery, *History and Christianity: a Vigorous, Convincing Presentation of the Evidence for a Historical Jesus*, Minneapolis, MN, Bethany, nd.

119. E. Basil Redlich, *Form Criticism*, Nelson & Sons, 1939 (cf. W. Wrede, *The Messianic Secret of the Gospels* (1901).

120. Charles C. Anderson, *Critical Quests of Jesus*, Grand Rapids, MI, Eerdmans, 1969.

121. Norman Geisler, *A General Introduction to the Bible*, Chicago, Moody Press, 1971, Rev.

122. Lord Chancellor Hailsham, "The Door Wherein I Went," *The Simon Greenleaf Law Review*, Vol 4, Orange, CA, The Simon Greenleaf School of Law, pp. 1-69.

123. Edmund H. Bennett, "The Four Gospels from a Lawyer's Standpoint," *The Simon Greenleaf Law Review*, Vol. 1, Orange, CA, The Simon Greenleaf School of Law, pp. 15-75.

124. J. N. D. Anderson, *Christianity: The Witness of History*, Downers Grove, IL, InterVarsity, 1970.